THE OFFICIAL
GRIMOIRE

A MAGICKAL HISTORY OF SUNNYDALE

WILLOW ROSENBERG

TEXT BY A. M. ROBINSON

TITAN BOOKS
London

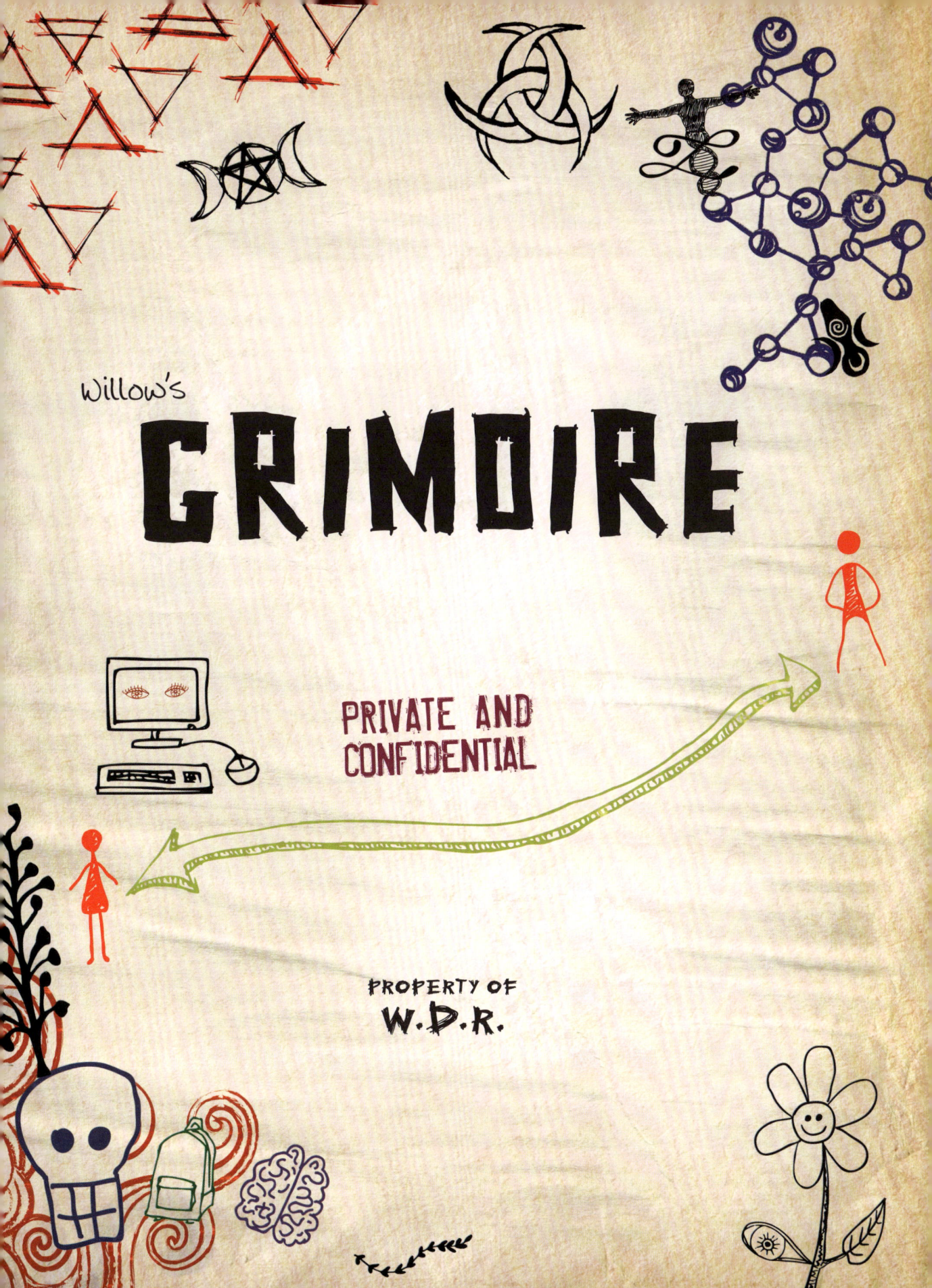

April 15, 2003

The First is coming. For the past few months, it's been playing with us, haunting us with the ghosts of our past and killing potential Slayers. There's still so much we don't understand, but we do know three things:

It's the greatest evil we have ever faced.

It won't rest until the Slayer line is dead.

We don't know how to stop it.

While I never intended these pages to be seen by any eyes other than my own, I've decided that I need to share the information with my friends, just in case I've missed something that will help us against the First, or—and I know no one wants to say it, but it needs to be said—in case I can't control the dark magick that I must call upon.

I love you all, no matter what.

P.S. Just a friendly reminder that if you need to make notes in the margins, use a nice, old-fashioned black pen. And if you happen to be the person who always eats Cheezy Poofs—not naming names, but you know who you are—please wash your hands before touching anything. And be gentle. The pages are fragile, and while I know book crimes are not the biggest evil we're facing, they're on the list.

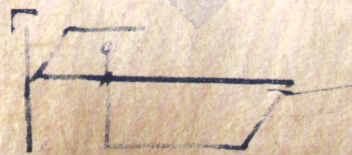

Bide the Wiccan Law ye must
In perfect love, in perfect trust.
Eight words the Wiccan Rede fulfill:
An ye harm none, do as ye will
And ever mind the rule of three:
What ye send out, comes back to thee.
Follow this with mind and heart,
And merry ye meet, and merry ye part.

> Before you say anything, yes, I made a Table of Contents for my personal grimoire. It's to help people use it as a reference. You're lucky it's not color-coded.
> —Willow

CONTENTS

BASIC TOOLS OF WITCHCRAFT
(That You Can Find Around the House)
10

RITUAL OF RESTORATION
(Or, A Spell to Return Angel's Soul)
12

SPELLS FOR BEGINNERS
(Levitating Feathers, Removing Zits, Etc.)
14

DE-LUSTING SPELL
(This Would Have Worked If Spike Hadn't Locked Me and Xander in the Factory)
16

AMY'S LOVE SPELL
(Xander On That Spell That Made Me Go After Him With An Axe)
17

A SPELL OF PROTECTION AGAINST OTHERWORLDLY FORCES
(But Not Against Almost Being Burned at the Stake by a Mob of Humans Being Manipulated by Otherworldly Forces)
20

DE-RATTING SPELL: ATTEMPT NUMBER ONE
(Amy Is Still a Rat)
22

A SPELL TO UNDERSTAND CATS
(But Only in Commercials)
23

A SPELL TO BIND THE HELLMOUTH SPAWN
(Or, How to Celebrate Your Third Apocalypse and the Return of the Octopus-Worm-Dragon-Looking Thing)
25

RITUAL TO RETRIEVE AN OBJECT FROM ANOTHER DIMENSION
(Like, Say, Your Vampire Doppelgänger)
27

A SPELL TO REMOVE WARDS FROM A PROTECTED OBJECT
(Note: Will Not Stop You From Being Kidnapped by the Mayor)
30

BREATH OF THE ATROPYX
(Oz and Xander Get Their Magic On)
31

DE-RATTING SPELL: ATTEMPT NUMBER TWO
(Hey! Maybe Amy Likes Being a Rat)
32

ARADIA'S GUIDING SPELL
(And Other Failed Attempts to Escape a Demonic Frat House)
37

THE WHEEL OF THE YEAR AND THE SABBATS
(Spoiler: You Celebrate Abundance. A Lot.)
38

SCRYING TOOLS
(For the Only Wiccan at UC Sunnydale)
41

HEX FOR A BROKEN HEART
(To Punish a Cheating Werewolf)
43

A SPELL TO ENACT ONE'S WILL
(Or, Budget Wedding Planning for Your Friend Buffy and Her... Spike)
45

BUFFY AND SPIKE'S WEDDING
46

ON COMBINING MAGICKAL ENERGIES
(Tara, and Spells for Two)
48

CHAKRAS
51

SIMPLE CONE OF POWER
52

TEST FOR SYNCHRONICITY
(Or, A Spell to Weaponize Roses)
52

A SPELL TO IONIZE THE AIR
(And Protect Spike from the Initiative Because... It Made Sense at the Time)
54

A SPELL TO LOCATE DEMONIC ACTIVITY IN SUNNYDALE
(Spoiler: It's Everywhere)
56

A SPELL TO JOURNEY INTO THE NETHERWORLD
(Or, How to Tell If Someone Has Stolen Your Friend's Body)
59

DRACONIAN KATRA SPELL
(Or, Reversing Faith's Buffy Bodysnatch)
60

THE SPELL OF THE PARAGON
(Giles on the Alternate Universe of Jonathan Levinson)
62

A TECHNIQUE TO KEEP YOUR INNER COOL
(Oz on Not Wolfing Out)
65

THE ENJOINING RITUAL
(Giles Has a Lot of Gourds)
68

SUPER-SLAYER SUMERIAN SPELLS
(Buffy on Fighting Adam)
70

DE-RATTING SPELL: ATTEMPT NUMBER THREE
(I Bought Amy a New Wheel)
73

REVERSING DEMONIC SPELLS
(Or, Popping Two Xanders Back Together)
75

CLOUTIER'S TRANCE
(A Spell to Spot the Presence of Magick at Work, Potentially in the Form of Your Sister)
77

SOBEKIAN BLOODSTONE MAGICK
(Anya on What Not to Sell to Hellgods)
78

SIMULATED SUNLIGHT SPELL
(Advanced Slaying Tools)
81

SPELLS TO FIGHT A TROLL
(Disarm a Troll, Send a Troll to Another Dimension—There's a Lot You Can Do with Trolls)
82

SPELLS TO FIGHT A HELLGOD
(Protection Spells, Teleportation Spells)
85

DE-INVITATION SPELL
89

A RESURRECTION SPELL
(Still a Bad Idea)
91

SPELLS TO CAUSE PAIN
(Dark Magick)
92

A BARRIER SPELL
(Protecting Against Horse-Riding Pursuors)
97

MINDWALKING
(Or, Snapping a Friend Out of an Ill-Timed Catatonia)
99

A SPELL TO REVERSE MIND ENERGY
(Getting Tara's Memories Back from Glory)
101

BRINGING BUFFY BACK
(A Spell to Call an Innocent Creature for Sacrifice and the Invocation of Osiris)
103

A SPELL TO MAKE A DISEMBODIED SPIRIT CORPOREAL
(So Buffy Can Kill It)
107

A MAGICKAL HISTORY OF THE EVIL TRIO
(Andrew on Glamours, Time Loops, and Demon Summoning)
108

TABULA RASA
(A Spell for Forgetting)
115

A SPELL FOR SUMMONING YOUR OWN PIT OF HELL
116

DE-RATTING SPELL: ATTEMPT NUMBER FOUR
(Success!)
118

A SPELL TO NOT DO SPELLS ANYMORE
(Yes, I Know. Let's Just Not Talk About This One)
121

SPELLS TO END THE WORLD
(Generally Avoid)
124

BLESSING OF GAIA
(Earth Magick and Forgiveness)
135

HEALING SPELL
(To Recover from Being Attacked by Gnarl)
137

A SPELL TO SUMMON A DEMON VIA THE USE OF A TALISMAN
(D'Hoffryn)
139

A SPELL TO REVERSE A PERSON'S GENDER
(R.J., or, Yet Another Love Spell Goes Awry)
141

A SPELL TO LOCATE THE FIRST EVIL
(Followed by Staying Very Far Away from the First Evil)
144

HOW TO PARALYZE AN ANCIENT EVIL
(Fighting the Turok-Han)
147

A SPELL TO LOCATE A POTENTIAL SLAYER
(As Written by Dawn)
150

THE RITUAL OF REVERSE EXCHANGE
(Or, What to Do After Your Slayer Jumps into a Portal)
155

A SPELL TO MAKE ONE SUSCEPTIBLE TO SUGGESTION
(As If Sunnydale's Police Force Didn't Have Enough to Deal With)
157

A SPELL TO GIVE VOICE TO ONE WHO CANNOT SPEAK
(Or, If You're Going to Kidnap Someone for Information, Make Sure They Have a Tongue)
159

A SPELL TO SHARE THE POWER OF THE CHOSEN ONE
(Magick with Slayer Scythes)
160

JUNE 15, 1998

I've never been good at keeping journals; the last time I tried was in second grade, and I stopped after Xander found it and asked why I had scribbled "Willow Harris" all over the back cover. But with Buffy gone, Angel dead, and everyone still kind of reeling, I could use a place to write things down.

Ever since I tried to do the ritual to restore Angel's soul, I've felt . . . different. I can't really put my finger on exactly how, but sometimes, when my mind's drifting as I wait to fall asleep, I'll suddenly feel something tugging at the edges of my consciousness.

Giles called our house the other day (and if you think he's all British and polite in person, you should hear him over the phone). He asked how I had been feeling, and I almost told him that he had been right: Attempting the Ritual of Restoration had opened a door. I mean, maybe not a full-size door, but definitely a pet door for a small poodle, or a magickal mail slot of some kind. But then I remembered that the spell was a big fat F, and it felt crazy to complain about side effects when the main event was such a failure.

I've decided that I'm just going to keep the whole witchcraft weirdness thing to my chest for a while and do a little research. I borrowed some books from the Sunnydale High library (see below), and have been checking out some of the sites that Miss Calendar used to visit. Besides, what else am I going to do? My best friend is missing, Xander is still being gross about Cordelia, and in between summer school, Dingoes gigs, and getting wolfy, Oz hasn't had that much time to hang.

Most of all, though, I can't stop thinking that if I'd done this research earlier, if I had spent more time going over Miss Calendar's spells and notes, if I had been a full-on witch rather than just an amateur—maybe the ritual would have worked and Buffy wouldn't have left. Maybe we would all be hanging at the Bronze, talking about how Angel is dealing with not being Angelus anymore.

So, this is not going to be a journal. It's going to be my Book of Shadows. My Grimoire. A Sunnydale Grimoire. And if Buffy comes back—please, Buffy, come back—I will be stronger.

Turns out you were rocking the full-on witch from the beginning. Sorry I took so long to deliver the memo. —B

That's my Will— the only lady I know who cites things voluntarily. —B

I cite things voluntarily. —G

Lady. "Only lady." No one is revoking your "I Was a Librarian" card. —B

Works Cited:

DeLauren, Aphrodisia. *Witchcraft*. London, UK: Moon Press, 1972. Print.

Montgomery, Nigel. *The Pagan Rites*. Chicago, IL: Mandrake Publishing, 1952. Print.

DiPastori, Thomas. *History of Witchcraft*. New York, NY: New Dawn Publications, 1961. Print.

Hebron (?). *Hebron's Almanac*. A Hellmouth: Some Guy Named Hebron Press, Really Old. Print.

Some of these? . . . Not so easy to get citation-y with. —W

BASIC TOOLS OF WITCHCRAFT
(THAT YOU CAN FIND AROUND THE HOUSE)

According to Aphrodisia DeLauren's <u>Witchcraft</u>, the first step in practicing Wicca is to decide what kind of witch you want to be. I'm thinking less of an Amy's-mom, set-cheerleaders-on-fire variety, and more of a love-the-earth, do-unto-others-as-you-would-kind-of-like-done-unto-you kind.

I've been working on gathering materials and setting up an altar in the center of my bedroom, but while I've gone to Sunnydale's magic shop, a teenage allowance gets one only so far. Until someone opens Ye Olde Dollar Shop of Magick, I think I'm going to have to improvise.

ATHAME
Used for directing energy during spells, the athame is often interchangeable with a sword, as both can be linked to the element of fire and are phallic in nature (for a religion that celebrates the ladies, it can sometimes be a phallus fest).

I know that it's ideal to make your own, but I'm not exactly a shop-class kind of girl. I found this at a Sunnydale garage sale. Seems legit?

This poisoned almost-cheerleader thanks you. —B

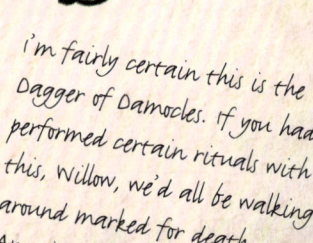

I'm fairly certain this is the Dagger of Damocles. If you had performed certain rituals with this, Willow, we'd all be walking around marked for death. Americans. —G

CAULDRON

Or, an old iron pot from the back of the cupboard. If I squint, it definitely screams, "I represent femininity and the Goddess and also make a nice vegetable soup."

CENSER

Good for witches who have maybe had one too many accidents with the makeshift incense holder. When calling upon a deity, place the censer in front of his or her image, but be sure to keep it a respectable distance from the curtains.

PENTACLE

Nabbed this from the library when Giles was arguing with Buffy about whether "slayhappy" was a word. It has the traditional pentagram, the five points of which represent the five elements: air, water, earth, fire, and spirit. Poor little pentagram—so misunderstood. You're not a Satanist symbol at all . . . Well, at least not when you're right side up.

Totally is. —B

I—still—beg to differ. —G

CHALICE

Good for mixing potions in modest quantities (and for drinking from when your parents are away at conferences and everything else in the kitchen is dirty).

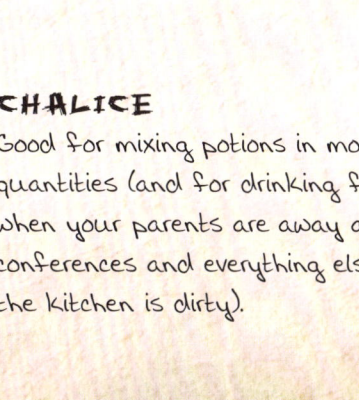

RITUAL OF RESTORATION
(OR, A SPELL TO CURSE A VAMPIRE WITH HIS SOUL)

I've gone over this three hundred times—it should have worked. I mean, okay, so I've never officially taken Latin and there was the whole head injury thing, but I've tested Miss Calendar's translation algorithm and cross-referenced the details with books on Romani rituals and her cyber-coven, and it checks out. Should I have attempted the Romani? Was the grave dirt not grave-y enough? Or maybe I left something out at the end; to be honest, it all gets a little bit fuzzy after "I call on you . . ."

TOOLS AND INGREDIENTS:
- RED SILK
- FOUR WHITE CANDLES (contained in glass)
- RUNIC TABLETS
- GRAVE DIRT

ORB OF THESULAH

I do believe I still need this back. It made a wonderful paperweight. —G

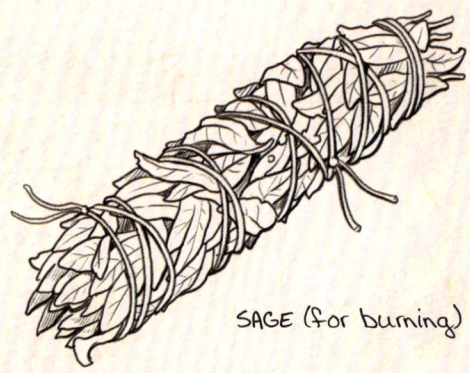

SAGE (for burning)

ANIMAL BONES

DIRECTIONS:

Draw a sacred circle—about two feet in diameter—with dirt taken from a fresh grave, then anchor one white candle at each of the four cardinal directions. Position the Orb of Thesulah on a bed of red silk at the circle's central point. After lighting the candles, place the animal bones so that they fill the remaining space.

Cleanse the air with burning sage. Begin the ritual by casting runes.

Then say:

> Quod perditum est, invenietur.
>
> Nici mort, nici al fiintei,
>
> Te invoc spirit al tercerii
>
> Zeii, se leagă de el. În rolurile principale inima din domeniul rău.
>
> Lasă-l să cunoască durerea umanită ii, zei.
>
> Ajunge la mâinile tale bătrân pentru mine. Dă-mi sabia.
>
> Te implor, Doamne; nu ignora aceasta rugăminte
>
> Nâsa orbită să fie vasul care-i vă transportă sufletul la el.
>
> Este scris, această putere este dreptul poporului meu să mânuiască.
>
> Redă trupului ce separe omul de animal
>
> Cu aiutorul acestui magic glob de cristal
>
> Asa să fie! Asa să fie!
>
> Acum! Acum!

TRANSLATION:

> What is lost, return.
>
> Not dead, nor of the living
>
> Spirits of the interregnum, I call.
>
> Gods, bind him, cast his heart from the evil realm.
>
> Let him know the pain of humanity, gods.
>
> Reach your wizened hands to me. Give me the sword.
>
> I call on you, Lord; do not ignore this request.
>
> Let this orb be the vessel that will carry his soul to him.
>
> It is written, this power is my people's right to wield.
>
> Return to the body what separates man from animal.
>
> So shall it be with the help of this magick crystal globe.
>
> So it shall be! So it shall be!
>
> Now! Now!

Alternate translation:
I implore you, God of Mopey Gits: Do not forsake your most willing servant.
He's neither interesting, nor overly dynamic.
Nevertheless, this orb is the vessel through which a poof must be restored,
I guess. I guess. —G

You have a soul now, too, you know. —B

Mine came from a cave demon. Night and bloody day. —G

SPELLS FOR BEGINNERS

I've tried a few small spells, which have been hit-and-miss. I'd give myself an A+ when it comes to levitation and blemish removal... and maybe an F when it comes to locator spells that don't blow power out for the entire block or séances that don't make it feel like you're being torn down the middle. But you know what they say: If at first you don't succeed, buy a new bedspread so your mother doesn't ask any questions.

LEVITATION SPELL △

(A SPELL FOR GAINING CLARITY AND EMOTIONAL CONTROL. ALSO TO, YOU KNOW, PICK STUFF UP.)

TOOLS AND INGREDIENTS:
- SAGE
- CLEAR QUARTZ CRYSTAL (aka rock crystal)
- SALT
- WHITE FEATHER

DIRECTIONS:
It's a good idea to cleanse your altar space with sage before beginning.

Using salt, draw an air symbol large enough to surround a practitioner who is seated with his or her knees crossed. Once seated within the symbol's confines, place the crystal on the line of the symbol in front of you, and the white feather beyond that. The feather should be partially visible through the crystal's translucence.

Focus your energies through the crystal toward the feather, imagining it lifting toward the ceiling. Once you have harnessed these energies, you will no longer need to do the full ritual, and can also move on to larger objects.

You could also just say "Light as a feather, stiff as a board." —D

BOOM! Floating No. 2s. What's next? No. 4s?! Wait, does anyone use those? —W

BEAUTY SPELL

(OR, HOW TO MAKE YOUR OWN MAGICKAL ZIT CREAM)

TOOLS AND INGREDIENTS:
- WHITE CANDLES (3)
- BOWL OF STILL WATER
- HONEY OPAL (to help get all confident with your bad self... too sassy?)
- ROSE PETALS

DIRECTIONS:
When the moon is new, sit by the light of three white candles that have never before seen flame. A bowl of still water should rest in front of you, the honey opal fully submerged. While sprinkling rose petals across the water's surface, say:

> **POWER OF ROSE, POWER OF MOON**
> **GRANT SKIN'S GLOW YOUR**
> **HEAVENLY BOON**

Remove the honey opal from the water and hold over the offending blemish. It should be gone the next morning.

This totally works! —D
Great! Remember this moment the next time you ask me to drop fifty dollars at the drugstore. —B

November 24, 1998

Buffy came back to Sunnydale a few months ago. At first it was weird. I mean, one, there was the whole reanimated zombie party that we ended up hosting, but also... I spent all summer waiting for her to come back, and when she finally did, all I felt was angry that she had left. We've talked a little, and it feels better, but I still don't know that everything is back to normal. There are some things I just don't know how to tell her. Like how, after years of hoping that Xander would finally look at me and go "Hey Wil! You're not just handy with a math equation, you're also a girl, with girl parts and a girl face that I would like to kiss," it's finally happened. Xander, the guy who fell for a praying mantis, a mummy girl, a reptile girl, an unavailable Slayer girl, and, worst of all, the mean cheerleader girl, has decided that the always-there-in-a-pinch friend girl is the one he'd like to date. He couldn't have figured this out before I had a cool guitarist boyfriend? One whose stoicism is matched only by his generosity in themed Pez dispensers? Oh, and have I mentioned that all of us—Xander, Cordelia, me, Oz—are supposed to go on a bowling double date?

I'd be lying if I said I hadn't fantasized about what Cordelia's face might look like if she caught us kissing. There we all are, standing by the water fountain, and I am leaning over to take a drink, and suddenly, she and Xander are behind me. Cordelia starts to open her dumb snarky mouth to say something, but before she can say, "Wow Willow, I didn't know corduroys came in such a rainbow of terrible colors" or "Make sure to say hi to Betsey at the Salvation Army the next time you see her!," Xander grabs me and kisses me, not caring that my lips still taste a little bit of Sunnydale High's funky water supply. (Also, I should state that I have normal, not water fountain-themed fantasies. Like homecoming! I have totally normal homecoming fantasies, where everything tastes like punch.)

But this can't happen. I like Oz; Oz likes me. And Oz has seen me this way from the beginning, not just because I'm suddenly dating someone else. These Xander feelings have to go away. I'm a little nervous about trying a love spell, but I've looked over Xander's notes on Amy's magick, and it's clear that her intent was about as pure as... a super-unpure thing. I truly, purely want these feelings to go away before we end up hurting anyone (even stupid Cordelia).

DE-LUSTING SPELL
(Based on DeLauren's Witchcraft)

A spell to remove inappropriate feelings between two friends who are dating other people. Maybe if one of them thought the other was so cool, he could have gotten his act together a little sooner.

TOOLS AND INGREDIENTS:
- ESSENCE OF ROSE THORN
- CONTAINER MADE OF GLASS
- MORTAR AND PESTLE
- OPEN FLAME
- BLACK CANDLES (3)

RAVEN FEATHERS
(one for each de-lustee)

SKINK ROOT
(this kind of did smell like butt)

DIRECTIONS:
By the light of three black candles, grind skink root and raven feathers together into a fine powder. Add four drops of essence of rose thorn to a glass container full of water. Bring to a boil.

When a steady steam is present, add the mixture of skink root and raven feather. While breathing in the resultant vapor, chant:

> **Goddess Badhbh, come thee hither,**
> **Make the love that bloomed now wither.**
> **As lungs fill, heart goes black,**
> **Let what once was solid crack.**

I knew Badhbh! Nice woman, at least as far as harbingers of doom go. I never believed that "furious rain of fire" thing. More her sister Macha's style.
—A

AMY'S LOVE SPELL

A certain red-haired temptress with whom I share a Bunsen burner said that if I wrote down the details of the spell Amy did for me last year for her new, secret book of witchy-woo, she would finish our chemistry project. Even if I hadn't forgotten to do my part of it last night, I would have said yes, for it is a well-known fact that when Will says "Jump!" the Xandman asks "How high?" When Will says "Roll!" the Xandman asks "Why?"—but then also "How fast?" And when she says, "Xander, you are going to run out of paper if you don't start writing about the spell." he says, "How right you are."

Let me just say that I know that I was wrong to ask Amy to do this. It's just, Cordelia dumped me on Valentine's Day, and there were hormones and bad decisions all around. In my defense, I never thought anyone would end up all ax-happy. I see now the error of my ways. From here on out, I will rely entirely on cologne stolen from my Uncle Rory and the kind of charm that gently wears a girl down over the course of many years.

Oh right, the spell. So parts of it are fuzzy—as a rule, I generally try to block out any memories where I am naked and shivering on the floor of a high school classroom, but hey. First time for everything.

"Xandman"? ...Oh, please. —G

Okay, "SPIKE." Or should I say, He who has called himself "The Big Bad" in the third person. Go fall on something spiky. —X

It's the cologne called Desperation. —A

HOW TO MAKE ME (XANDER) IRRESISTIBLE:
1. Take a big old creepy jar of chicken blood and paint the symbol for the Lilith Fair on the ground (or, as I have just been informed, the universal symbol for womanhood and femininity. I knew that).
2. Have the love-ee (meaning me) strip down to some stylish yet roomy sleep pants and sit in the middle of the symbol, holding a lit black candle and looking at Cordelia's glamour shot.
3. Enlist a clearly unqualified witch to put ingredients—a lot of oils and essences (which smell like butt), some sort of leaf thing, and a locket you spent way too much money on—in a glass beaker while saying:

    Diana, Goddess of Love and the Hunt,
    I pray to thee, let my cries bind the heart of Xander's beloved.
    May she neither rest nor sleep until she submits to his will.
    Diana, bring about this love and bless it.

4. Blow out the black candle.

Figuring out some of Amy's ingredients is pretty hard. Chicken blood is normally used in curses, and if the oils and essences used really "smelled like butt," as Xander reports, I'm thinking it's coming from the darker aisles of the magick shop. Clearly having her picture in the circle protected Cordelia, but then what role did the locket play? It must have had sentimental value to Cordelia, and the spell magnified and shared those feelings with Sunnydale's womenfolk... or Amy just wanted to burn something Cordelia cared about. Let's just stay away from blood and personal objects in this de-lusting spell. —Willow

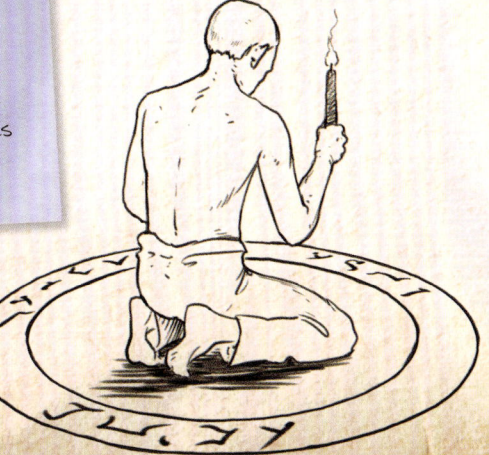

JANUARY 12, 1999

Buffy's birthday is coming up, and she's worried it's going to be like all her other birthdays and end with badness. I tried to reassure her that this one was going to be the normalest of normal, boring even—after all, I told her, so much has already happened with Spike taking us hostage, Cordelia getting hurt, Xander and I realizing we didn't want to be together, and that whole First Evil thing trying to get Angel to kill himself (again).

However, between you and me . . . she's cursed. The other night, on patrol, she discovered the bodies of two children. Even worse, it happened to be the <u>one</u> night that Joyce decided to tag along.

Joyce . . . is taking it hard. Sunnydale is taking it hard. I mean, that's good! That is an appropriate response to, you know, the whole murder thing; every time I see the photos of those kids in the newspaper or on bulletin boards, I have to go through the list of people we've saved since Buffy came to town to stop from curling up into a tiny ball. But for a town that has a tendency to say, "Gee! Another spontaneous neck rupture! Who'da thunk?!," this feels . . . strange. They even held a candlelight vigil at the town hall last night, where Mayor Wilkins gave a speech.

But the weirdest thing? My mom went. Somehow, this pulled Sheila "I Would but I Have a Paper up for Review Next Month" Rosenberg out of her study. The first time I came home from school crying because Cordelia was mean to me, she handed over a tissue, then asked if

I could give her a rough estimate of what percentage of our student body had ever experienced adolescent bullying. She's never really been Miss Let Me Show You My Parental Concern.

Tonight, when we were driving home after the vigil, a part of me wanted to tell her everything. Like about how I have been practicing witchcraft. Or about how I am dating an amazing (and thankfully very forgiving) musician, and how, for the first time in maybe forever, I'm feeling comfortable being Willow. But then she started talking about how, my friend "Bunny" was evidencing the typical microaggressions of a girl without any stable male role model, and the moment passed.

Anyway, Buffy. What better gift for the Slayer who has everything than a protection spell from an enthusiastic amateur witch who has at least a 50—hey, maybe 60!—percent chance of actually succeeding? My books say that protection spells work best if they are performed with others, so I've called Michael and Amy and Amy's real cauldron. I've designed it to guard specifically against supernatural harm, because yay specificity! But if it also creates a bonus protection cloud that guards anyone who happens to be in a car in which my supernatural friend Buffy is the driver? Not going to complain.

A SPELL OF PROTECTION
AGAINST OTHERWORLDLY FORCES
(AND MAYBE BUFFY'S DRIVING)

This is a spell to protect Buffy from the kind of birthday guests who crashed last year's party. Like a humanity-hating demon and a suddenly evil significant other.

I repeat—have you considered not celebrating your birthday? —G

Hey! I've gotten better. If it wasn't for that possessed mailbox, I would have totally passed the last test. —B

TOOLS AND INGREDIENTS:

DRIED CLOVES

PAGAN BEADS
(made from bloodstone, or another protective mineral)

SKULL OF ONE KILLED BY SUPERNATURAL BEING
(Amy says she has one of these from a website, and it came with a "certificate of 100% verified demon murder." Yikes.)

HENBANE
(Remove roots—use only the leaves and flowers.)

BLACK CANDLES (3)

Just a friendly reminder that the Magic Box will price-match any item you find on the internet. Or, at least, it would have. —A

CAULDRON

Directions:

Draw symbol of protection on the ground; place your active (meaning filled with boiling water) cauldron in its center. By the light of three black candles, make an offering to the goddess Thalia by placing bloodstone beads in the skull.

Form a circle with two fellow practitioners, and add dried henbane and cloves to the boiling water. Once the mixture's scent can be detected in the air, clasp hands and focus energy on the person or object you would like to protect from demonic or otherworldly interference. Say the following in unison:

Goddess Thalia, goddess divine,

Guard well this friend of thine.

Guard from spirit, guard from beast,

Guard from demon until the moon has passed.

DE-RATTING SPELL
ATTEMPT NUMBER ONE

Funny story. You know how I said that Sunnydale had gone a little bonkers after those two little kids were murdered? Well, turns out they weren't really "two little kids" and were more "one big grouchy demon" whose hobby was blowing into small towns and inspiring witch hunts. Question—if a mob of angry townspeople attempts to burn you at the stake, does that give you more witch cred, or less? I'm thinking more.

Luckily, Giles was able to expose the demon before anyone ended up flambéed. Amy didn't let it get to this point, though, and turned herself into a rat, which is starting to look like something of a go-to spell for her.

I've tried everything, but I can't seem to figure out the rat-i-dote; animal transmogrification is a few magickal grades above me. Now she's sitting on my bedspread and twitching her little pink nose at me as I try to find the right mix of herbs to go along with the incantation that Amy used to de-rat Buffy after Xander's love spell went awry.

DIANA, HECATE, I HEREBY LICENSE THEE TO DEPART.

GODDESS OF CREATURES GREAT AND SMALL, I CONJURE THEE TO WITHDRAW.

... Maybe I should get a wheel thing and a cage just in case this takes a little longer than I thought. A week as a cute little whiskery thing isn't going to hurt anyone, right? And—silver lining!—I've been stumbling across some new spells in the process.

Ooh, does this mean I have witch cred, too? What do I get? Is it a like a punch card or one of those point systems? —B

A Spell to Understand Cats
(But Only in Commercials)

Tools and Ingredients:

- Iron plate
- Mortar and pestle
- Catnip
- Valerian
- Cat's claw (the herb, not from an actual cat)

Directions:

After one hasn't slept for a few days, and when one is very, very tired, grind together all the herbs until you have a fine powder. Sprinkle a dash of powder on the iron plate and say:

> **Diana, Hecate, I hereby license thee to impart.**

Throw a match onto the plate. There will be a flash, and for a short amount of time, you'll be able to understand that the tasty nibblets in the Tasty Nibblets commercial aren't all that well-liked by the cat actors. The spell doesn't seem to work on cats in person, though. Wonder why...

We're all pretty sure Willow was hallucinating here, right? All that herbal inhalation couldn't be good. —A

Without question. —G

January 26, 1999

Here's a fun question—how does one celebrate facing their third apocalypse? I mean, everybody knows that the first apocalypse (the Master) is the paper one, and the second (Acathla) is wood, but what's number three? Crystal? Cynicism? Good old-fashioned panic?

Pretty sure it's silver.—G

Giles let us know that the Sisterhood of Jhe ladies we fought the other day in the sewers are not part of a friendly demon book club, but members of an apocalypse cult who have figured out how to reopen the Hellmouth in the library. I still have nightmares about the first time the Hellmouth Spawn popped out, when Buffy was busy fighting the Master; I'm really not looking forward to seeing it or its tentacles again.

This time, however, I know that I can be of more help. Giles and I are working on the binding spell that will drive the Spawn back into the depths, and Buffy, Angel, and Faith are all preparing for the fight of their lives. The other day, when I was coming out of the magic shop with the ingredients, I ran into Xander and almost told him what was going on. But Buffy's right: With Xander's recent track record, it's better if he's fray-adjacent.

Hey! You know what? While you guys were doing your little binding spell, I was working a little magic of my own. Well, actually, this guy named Jack was working the magic, and it was less magic, and more Let Me Raise My Hillbilly Friends With a Desiccated Body Part I've Been Carrying Around on a String, but let the record show, I had my own stuff going on.—X

Now with twice as many tentacles!—W

A Spell to Bind the Hellmouth Spawn

(How to send that octopus-worm-dragon thing back to where it belongs... beneath the library)

Tools and Ingredients:

- Black candles (3)
- Red candles (15)
- White candles (15)
- Blood of beast

Directions:

With the blood of an animal that walks with four feet on the ground, paint the binding symbol on the earth where the beast is predicted to emerge. Place a group of candles—at least two, and of mixed colors for balance—at each point of both the inner and outer octagons.

While lighting the candles, say:

> Terra, vente, ignis et pluvial.
>
> Cuncta quattuor numina, vos obsecro.
>
> Defendite nos a recente malo resolute
>
> et omnia vasa veritatis!

Translation:

> Earth, wind, fire, and rain.
>
> All four powers, I beseech you.
>
> Protect us from fresh evil unleashed
>
> And all the vessels of truth!

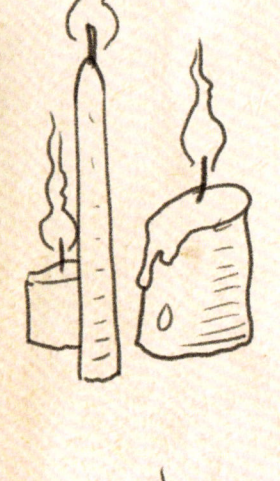

When the beast appears, continue your chant, repeating it one hundred times. On the end of the hundredth repetition, strike the beast, and it will be driven back into its earthly prison for good.

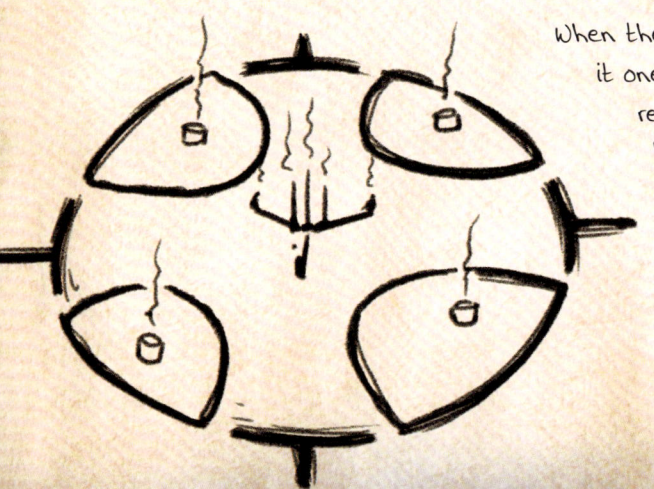

February 23, 1999

Someone should really make a sort of Dos and Don'ts list for beginning witches. I mean, I know there's the whole "I will live every day in Dignity, Courage, Honor, and Truth" thing, but there could also be some practical basics. For example, maybe:

- If a strange girl named Anya approaches you in the hallway and asks you to do a spell to find her lost necklace, just say no.

And speaking of "saying no," here's another thing that I should have nixed:

- Writing Percy West's history paper.

But I didn't say no, because that's not what Willow Rosenberg, the Reliable-Dog-Geyser Person, does. She does other people's homework and lets strangers trick her into doing spells that are clearly not as advertised.

When it became clear that Anya's spell wasn't just about bringing back a missing piece of jewelry, I stood up and walked out—and it felt good. While I'm still not sure exactly what the spell was supposed to do other than give me a sneak peek of hell's latest movie trailer, I'm writing down what we did just in case.

(Note: I'm not sure about the chicken feet; I just brought them as a kind of spell-warming present. Still working on the ins and outs of witch etiquette... Wait. You know what? Etiquette be damned! New Willow eschews all spell-warming gifts. She will just show up at your spells and eat all your mystical snacks.)

The other day I read that there were witches in the Middle Ages who used to bottle up their spit to give to other witches as one of the deepest sym[bols] of friendship and trust... Yes, I [am] a hit at parties. —[ ]

Never mind about that whole entry from before; it turns out that Anya's spell did bring something over from another dimension, it's just that that something was less of a necklace and more of an evil, fangy version of me in a <u>very</u> restrictive bustier. Vampire Me certainly wasn't a pushover, but she also had some issues, including being entirely demented.

Still... I can't deny that the lady knew how to get results.

After she threatened him at the Bronze, Percy wrote his own history paper. He even gave me a copy, along with an apple. I mean, it's insane, and I'm kind of terrified now about the quality of my education given that he got a C+ on it, but he did it because Vampire Me didn't back down.

Maybe there is a nice midpoint between Fluffy Pushover Willow and Scary Dominatrix Willow—one who stands up for herself and eats bananas whenever she wants, but maybe doesn't kill so many people.

And she knew how to pull off green eyeshadow. —B

I know this one! It's Fluffy Dominatrix Willow.—X

RITUAL TO RETRIEVE AN OBJECT FROM ANOTHER DIMENSION
(IN THIS CASE, A NECKLACE—OR SO ANYA SAID)

TOOLS AND INGREDIENTS:

- CERAMIC PLATE (upon which one has drawn an image of the lost object)
- A BOTTLE OF PURPLE SAND

BONES, a lot of them (Anya brought these, and I didn't ask questions. A mix of mandibles and rib cages?)

> **EYRISHON**
>
> As a part of my new "Investigate Before You Supplicate" policy I went back and did a little research on this guy and his whole "Endless One" deal. He was the leader of a Kronos cult in the ninth century, but vanished one day without a trace. A few people have reported sightings over the years, but nothing's been confirmed. He's kind of like a time-bending Elvis.
> —Willow

PURPLE CANDLES

CHICKEN FEET (?)

DIRECTIONS:

By the light of purple candles, create a circle of bones. After placing the ceremonial plate in the center, the spellcasters should take a seat across from one another inside the circle. With palms facing up, have each practitioner extend a hand until their fingertips touch in the middle.

Then, offer supplication to Eyrishon, alternating who speaks from line to line.

EYRISHON. K'SHALA. MEH-UHN

DIPRECHT. DOH-TEHENLO NU-EYRISHON.

THE CHILD TO THE MOTHER.

THE RIVER TO THE SEA.

EYRISHON. HEAR MY PRAYER.

When a burst of rainbow-y white energy appears, slowly pour the sand through the supplicants' fingers. When the bottle is empty and the sand has emptied onto the plate, Eyrishon <u>should</u> have brought the lost object to you.

MAGIC BOX

These were some of the pages I took from the Books of Ascension in the Mayor's cabinet. Still don't know what most of it says.
—Willow

BOOKS OF ASCENSION

May 18, 1999

Nothing like getting kidnapped by an evil mayor-Slayer combo to give a girl a little clarity.

On one hand, it helped me decide that I belong in Sunnydale, fighting the good fight with my friends while proudly attending UC Sunnydale, a school that the U.S. News & World Report ranked only slightly better than sitting in your family's basement and taking online courses called "Make Money Writing from Home!!!!"

On the other, it made it very clear how unprepared we all are for Graduation Day. I saw the kind of magick the mayor has been doing, and I felt the dark power emanating from the Books of Ascension. It's made removing wards and getting all stabby on the mayor's goons with pencils seem like nothing. I can't even figure out how to fix Amy. The other day, I realized that I had started to think of her as a rat who only moonlights as human.

This morning, while looking for magick to stop the Ascension, I came across a spell for talking with ferns to help them grow all lush and fern-y. There was a footnote about how someone had once used it to turn their favorite fern into a human companion, and I thought there might be a way to adapt it so that I could turn Amy back. But all it did was give her long, lustrous rat whiskers.

Oz is going to be here any second, so I'm going to jot this down quickly, just in case. I don't know, maybe we luck out and the mayor turns into something with whiskers. Or something that has an irrational fear of whiskers; there are weirder demon phobias out there. I have to figure out how to act when Oz gets here—in typical Oz fashion, he said he'd just come over to hang, but is that even possible given what's looming around the corner? I feel like we need to be doing something bucket list-y, but I hate the outdoors, and Oz once told me he spends most of his movie watching just reworking the soundtracks in his head. Say, what's a good date idea when you've already gone to prom together but maybe only have two more days to live?

Obviously sex. —A

DE-RATTING SPELL
ATTEMPT NUMBER TWO
(OR, A SPELL TO GROW A RAT'S WHISKERS REALLY LONG)

TOOLS AND INGREDIENTS:

- RED STRING (about 1.5 feet)
- MANDRAKE ROOT
- WHITE CHALK

DIRECTIONS:

With white chalk, draw the symbol for rebirth on the ground. Place the object you want to transform in the center. Tie and knot one end of a red string around the top of a mandrake root, then hold the other end of the string so that the mandrake dangles above the object of your spell and makes small circles that mimic the direction of the chalked spiral.

**WHAT ONCE WAS STILL, NOW TRANSFORM.
LET MY FRIEND BE REBORN.**

BREATH OF THE ATROPYX

TOOLS AND INGREDIENTS:

A FOUR-HANDLED CAULDRON (placed on a pedestal [important!!])

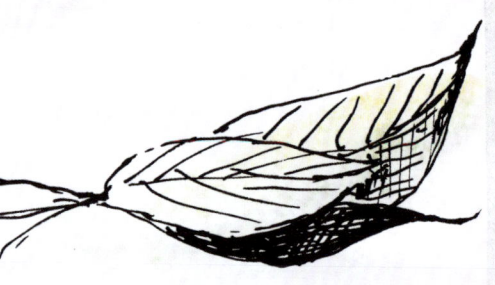

TWICE-BLESSED SAGE (three leaves, dried)

ESSENCE OF TOAD

(Note: Follow these instructions to the letter so we can destroy the box immediately when we get it back to the library. And, Xander, because I can already hear you asking what part of the toad the essence comes from—you don't want to know.)

Fill the cauldron with water (use the faucets in the girls' restroom, because you know the ones in the boys' can be iffy). After it's filled to at least the halfway point, put it on the wire pedestal in Giles's office. Add the three leaves of sage, followed by the essence of toad.

This mixture needs to steep for a minimum of two hours. When we bring the box back, we'll sprinkle the box with your toad tea, say some fancy words, and then that should destroy whatever is inside.

A Spell to Remove Wards from a Protected Object
(Adapted from DeLauren's Witchcraft)

Tools and Ingredients:

—SACRED SAND (from a location as close as possible to the warded object's origin—in this case, Central America)

Directions:
Sprinkle sand on the object whose wards you wish to remove. Before the last grain falls, say the following:

	Translation:
Sis modo resolutum	That which has been shielded
Exposco validum scutum.	Shall be paralyzed.
Diutus nec defende	Lay down your weapons
A manibus arcum intende.	And defend yourself no longer.

March 16, 1999

We've learned that Faith has teamed up with Mayor Wilkins and formed a big mean weirdly smiley evil team. I never trusted her! Well, okay, maybe I did a little at the beginning when I was seduced by alligator wrestling stories, but after that, not a fan. We knew that she was hanging on by a thread after she accidentally killed the deputy mayor, but we never expected it to go this far.

Now she's helping the mayor prepare for something called the Ascension. I've been hitting the books with Giles all week, but we still don't know all the details—just that it's going to happen on Graduation Day and that he's going to turn into something 1) less than human and 2) less than fun.

In order to do so, he's going to need whatever is in the box that showed up at the docks the other day. We're going to try to perform the Breath of the Atropyx on whatever's inside—I'm assuming some sort of demon gummy vitamins—but first I'm going to need to remove any and all magickal protections. Unfortunately, that's kind of an up-close-and-personal process, so while we're doing that at City Hall, Xander and Oz are going to be working the Breath mojo in the library. I've left them very clear instructions, but am still a little nervous.

Speaking of things that make me nervous . . . Yesterday, the last of my college acceptance letters arrived. I got into every school that I applied to, including Harvard, Oxford, and MIT. But when I started to think about what my life would be like if I said yes to any of those places, I couldn't picture it. A part of me didn't want to picture it. How could I just move away and take Introduction to Philosophy or Literature of the Cretaceous Period like none of this ever happened? Like I didn't know that there was a Hellmouth in California just waiting to burst open? That I'd left Buffy and Xander and Giles alone on the front lines?

I guess I shouldn't worry about it. This could all be a whole lot of moot pending Ascension.

C+ There were some facts buried in here. You can graduate.

Percy West
US History (Fourth Period)
Mr. Morrigan

THEODORE ROOSEVELT

Theodore Roosevelt was a man. A president man. But not that other president—his name was Franklin, and if you want to know about him you should read the other report I wrote for Rosenberg, because I wasn't sure which one I was supposed to write it about.

Anyway, Theodore Roosevelt was born in 1858, which was a long time ago. Even though he was old, he became the twenty-sixth president of the United States. As a kid he had asthma, which was a bummer, but he played a lot of sports and stuff and it got better. He even joined a gang called the Rough Riders, which is a good name, but not, you know, next-level good. Later, he started another gang that he called the Bull Moose Party. Personally, I think that was a step backward in the naming department, but no one wanted to tell him because of that time he got shot in the chest before giving a speech, and he still went up and gave it. He was hardcore.

When he was president, he passed a lot of acts, or whatever they're called. He liked the outdoors so he turned a lot of places into national monuments, including Muir Woods, which is a really boring place full of trees that you have to go to on family vacations. So, thanks for that, Teddy. Oh, and his nickname was Teddy, but he hated when people called him that, because he didn't like people knowing that at night he sometimes turned into a teddy bear. . . . *The Hellmouth really does warp you.—D*

Anyway, I think that's it. I couldn't remember what the word count of this report was supposed to be, and I couldn't call Rosenberg because I didn't want to disturb her again in the middle of her Goth chick moment, which is a valid lifestyle choice for which I have nothing but respect.

Peace.

Kind of wigged out now about only getting a "C" in this class.—B

GRADUATION CEREMONY ENDS IN TRAGEDY

Sunnydale High School Demolished

What began as a joyous occasion ended in tragedy on Tuesday afternoon, when the latest in a series of gas leaks at Sunnydale High School proved to be fatal during its senior graduation ceremony. Soon after Mayor Richard Wilkins finished his commencement speech congratulating the class of '99, an explosion ripped through the campus. Officials believe that it began in the library, which was recently challenged for its non-traditional collection of reading material.

The blaze claimed the life of Sunnydale's beloved mayor, its high school principal, and dozens of students. Others are being treated at the local hospital for injuries and gas-related confusion. When pressed for comment, one student said "A snake! A big [expletive] snake. Hey, do you think I'm going to get my gown deposit back?"

Cue cards for Mayor Wilkins's speech were found among the wreckage. In honor of his legacy, the full transcript is included below.

Geez Louise, do we really have to sit through this again? It's the speech that won't die! —X
Evil. —B

Well. What a day this is! Special day. Today is our centennial—the one hundredth anniversary of the founding of Sunnydale, and I know what that means to all you kids: not a darn thing. Because today something more important happens: today you all graduate from high school. Today all the pain, all the work, all the excitement is finally over. And what's a hundred years of

October, 26, 1999

Good news! We all survived high school without becoming snake chow. Well, not all of us—we lost a lot of good classmates.

There were also all those books in the library that went kablooey. Luckily, I had borrowed a lot in my search for de-ratting/de-ascending spells, so Giles's collection wasn't totally lost. He's hard to read sometimes, but I could tell that he was happy to have them back, beneath all the "Willow, I appreciate your quest to increase your knowledge of magick, but you really do need to let me know what you are borrowing. I have a system."

I know that I haven't written—or, well, spelled—in a while, but there's been a lot going on. I feel like I am really rocking this whole matriculation business. After making twenty different potential schedules and then ranking them all according to difficulty, balance of subject matter, and sense of whimsy, I finally found the perfect mix. I even got Buffy to take Dr. Walsh's psychology class with me, but I don't think she's enjoying it. I don't think she's enjoying college that much at all. I get it. It must be hard dealing with Angel leaving, the demon roommate, poop-head Parker, and then poop-head Spike (who seems to always be lurking about) probably didn't help. And between hanging out with Oz and his friends, I haven't been able to be there for her as much as I've wanted. I should invite her out more, but given how often we end up heading to the Bronze to watch some random new band, it doesn't always seem like a recipe for cheering up.

> I wasn't lurking. I was plotting. It's a whole different vibe. —S

Sometimes, though, it seems like she's not even trying. Which makes what happened at the Alpha Delta house even more frustrating. I know I told her that everything was okay—and it's true that, compared to our deepest, darkest fears manifesting themselves and trying to kill us, the status quo is peachy. But she does treat me like her sidekick, one whose help she conveniently forgets about when she's feeling cranky. First it's all "Great job, Will, couldn't have done it without you!" and then, suddenly, she's like "Conjuring? Are you sure you're ready to lose the magickal training wheels?"

> Tell me about it. —D

> Will, you're so much more than a sidekick. And Dawn, you're not even allowed to be a sidekick. —B

I'll get over it, I know. And granted, the guiding spell didn't go so well in the Fear House, but can't we chalk that up to the whole demonic influence thing? (And yes, okay, some mild indecisiveness on my part.) But the only thing I can do is keep practicing so that my spells aren't always "fifty-fifty." I can't become a better witch if no one trusts me.

ARADIA'S GUIDING SPELL
(A SPELL TO LEAD YOU TO SOMEONE WHO IS LOST IN A CREEPY FRAT HOUSE OF DOOM)

DIRECTIONS:
Find a spot where you can be seated with legs crossed in the lotus position and hands resting on your knees, then say the following incantation:

> **ARADIA, GODDESS OF THE LOST.**
>
> **THE PATH IS MURKY. THE WOODS**
>
> **ARE DENSE. DARKNESS PERVADES.**
>
> **I BESEECH THEE... BRING THE LIGHT.**

A small green light—almost like a firefly—should appear. Inform it of the person or place that you seek, and it should lead the way.

Guess that's twenty dollars I won't get back. That bloke owed me money. —G

Actual size. —W

> **ARADIA**
> The mother of Italian witchcraft, sometimes also referred to as the Great Goddess, the Moon Goddess, or the Beautiful Pilgrim. She's said to have led a coven of fourteenth-century Diana-worshiping witches in Tuscany. Persecuted by the Roman Catholic Church, she left for parts unknown. Good to invoke for spells involving unexpected travel.
> —Willow

← AVOID DRAWING THIS... I mean, apart from right now. But maybe it's okay because Buffy smooshed the demon? I did some research, and it says it's activated by blood. If I get a paper cut, I'll just... go bleed on something else.

The Wheel of the Year and the Sabbats

YULE (OR WINTER SOLSTICE)
Occurring on the shortest day of the year in the Northern Hemisphere, it represents a time of renewal and hope. Consider spells with pine, which is often used to ward off illness, during this time. Pine is also associated with Dionysus, so... super appropriate for anyone attending UC Sunnydale.

Beer is good. —B

Last year I didn't celebrate any witchy holidays, and here we are, at Samhain, and I almost missed it all over again. If I'm going to really get over this plateau and make people respect my powers, I have to buckle down and get into the spirit of things. So, consider this my personal guidebook to the sabbats. I'm still trying to figure out which one is the one where I'm supposed to go to the movies and eat Chinese food.

SAMHAIN
Witch's New Year, celebrated from October 31 to November 1, is a time of death and rebirth. A good time to shed old habits and attitudes. Ideal for banishing spells and for making offerings to ancestors who have passed as the seen and unseen worlds collide.

AUTUMN EQUINOX (OR MABON)
The last spoke on the Wheel of the Year, this sabbat also honors abundance, but from a place of reflection. You go "Hey! Look at all that abunding we did this year!" (After a while, the festivals get a little similar.)

LUGHNASSAD (OR LAMMAS)
Lugh was said to be the older and wiser personification of the god Beil. Celebrated around the annual point when wheat would be harvested, this sabbat is a time for bread and beer (just not caveman beer). There's even an old ritual where a bean is added to the bread dough, and whoever gets the bean will be granted a wish (just not a vengeance wish).

BRIGID'S DAY (OR IMBOLIC)

Brigid, also referred to as Lady of the Flame or Goddess of the Heart, was a beloved Celtic goddess of healing, smithcraft, and poetry, and this sabbat, celebrated in early February, honors the divine powers of inspiration. So go and write that English paper, Willow!

SPRING EQUINOX (OR OSTARA)

Taking its name from a German fertility goddess, this sabbat was nabbed by Christians and turned into Easter. It's about the triumph of life over death, and finding balance, equality, and harmony. A good time for plant spells.

BELTANE

A sabbat to honor the god Beil, Beltane is another time to do magick that encourages fertility and a bountiful harvest. On this day (usually May 1), there will probably be a whole lot of boinking going on around the Maypole. Or Quad. Whatever is more appropriate to your situation.

SUMMER SOLSTICE

Celtic pagan mythology depicts this as the end of the Oak King's reign as he is overrun by the Holly King, who is said to preside over the waning part of the year. A sabbat to celebrate the bounty of Mother Nature, it can boost spells seeking abundance and wealth. Earth spirits are said to be out in greater force, so if you ever wanted to dial a faerie, maybe do it here.

No. Not on the Hellmouth, please. I'm asking this as a personal favor. Who knows what will pop out? —B

In general, faeries are a peaceful lot as supernatural beings go, but I agree. There are . . . concerns. —G

OCTOBER 31, 1999 (SAMHAIN)

They should have said, "Come Join the UC Sunnydale Group for People Who Bake and Bought Some Incense Once" on their fliers instead. The Wicca group seems to be light on the actual Wicca.

Last week I made the mistake of asking the Wicca group how everyone was planning to celebrate Samhain, and was met with fifteen blank looks. So I decided to make my own Samhain. A Samhain for One. For the uninitiated, it might have looked a lot like coming home to sit alone in your room while your boyfriend goes to see Veruca, his favorite Shirley Manson wannabe, in concert, but don't be fooled! It was a capital-"S" Sabbat.

If I were part of a real coven, we would have all danced around in a circle with drums and tambourines to honor the Horned God as the harvest ends and the winter season begins. But since it's slightly depressing to wear a horned helmet and talk to yourself . . . or so I've been told . . . and since I'm all out of cattle to bring down the mountain to slaughter this year, I thought it might be cool to take advantage of the weakened veil between the dead and living to focus on divination.

Cool? Can I add that this sounds a lot like the beginning of, oh, I don't know, every horror movie in the world?—X

. . . Freaky.—B

I know.—W

I tried a basic scrying ritual with a crystal ball. It worked . . . although I haven't been able to make heads or tails of what appeared. A white shirt covered in blood, a jagged tower bursting from the earth, a flash of myself with black hair. Not sure what it means—beware bad hair decisions?—but it felt prickly. Like a warning.

40

SCRYING TOOLS

TOOLS AND INGREDIENTS:
- ATHAME
- BLACK VELVET (or blanket or sheet)
- CANDLE (preferably purple or indigo)
- SANDALWOOD INCENSE

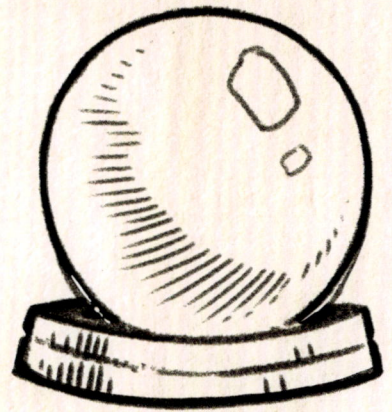

A CRYSTAL BALL
(free of imperfection)

DIRECTIONS:
Find a room that's quiet and dark except for the light of one candle. Cover a table or other surface with your black sheet or blanket and place the crystal ball on top; this will allow you to focus your gaze as you prepare to stare into its depths.

Cast a small circle about yourself with your athame, then close your eyes and envision yourself surrounded by a white light while making a silent request for the Goddess's protection.

When you open your eyes, peer into the crystal and keep your mind as blank as possible. Soon, you should see the ball fill with mist or smoke. When the haze disappears, it will leave a picture, one that will require interpretation, much like a dream.

NOVEMBER 9, 1999

Veruca is a werewolf. Oz slept with Veruca.

I've been staring at those two sentences for the last fifteen minutes, surrounded by ingredients that I've pulled out of the chest by my bed. Buffy said that I should put the blame where it belongs, but there are two names in those sentences.

How could I have been so stupid? Sitting next to him all those nights at the Bronze, asking him questions about the music when he was wrapped up in a web of werewolf attraction, wanting her. Dumb Willow, couldn't possibly understand, so instead of explaining what was happening, he let me find them together, naked, on the floor of that cage. And then he has the nerve to tell me that he knows what it feels like because once upon a time he saw me kiss Xander when I thought we were going to die.

I want them to feel as broken as I feel now. I want their hearts to wither, and for them to feel low, and unwanted, and full of hate.

I've never done a hex before, but I've read them. I've studied them. And I do have the power to do it.

Hex for a Broken Heart
(A Spell to Punish Lovers Who Have Strayed)

AGRIMONIA PILOSA (Original calls for Agrimonia, but I changed it to "hairy agrimony." Because werewolves.)

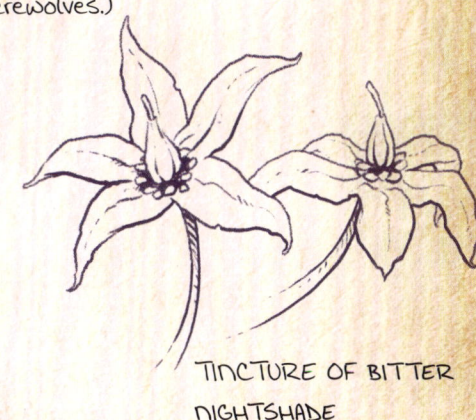

TINCTURE OF BITTER NIGHTSHADE

Tools and Ingredients:
- Objects representative of those you want hexed
- Cloth of rough fiber
- Lanolin
- Sap of the bloodwood tree (diluted)
- Raven feathers (enough to make a whole damned bird)

Directions:

Line the bottom of a bowl with your rough-fibered cloth and soak it with lanolin. Set it ablaze. Focus your hate to keep it burning.

While the flames are high, grind the agrimony and raven feathers into a fine powder. As you work, say the following:

> I conjure thee by Barabbas, by Satanas, and the Devil.
>
> As thou art burning, let Oz and Veruca's deceitful hearts be broken.
>
> I conjure thee by the Saracen queen and by the name of Hell.
>
> Let them find no love or solace, let them find no peace as well.
>
> Let this image seal his fate, not to love, only hate.

Upon completion of the incantation, burn the representative objects in the fire, then douse with the nightshade and sap. The hex will be complete when the flames are extinguished.

NOVEMBER 30, 1999

I couldn't go through with the hex on Oz. I got to the part of the spell where I was supposed to burn his picture, and then I stopped. The final ingredients were floating and ready to pour, but I saw that little half smile, and I knew I couldn't go through with it. ~~I wish I had.~~

I don't mean that. Not really. He saved me from Veruca... but then he left before we had a chance to talk about anything. Now he's gone, and all that's left are all these words I will never get to say and a jagged cloud of anger that builds and builds and builds in my chest. I don't even have his things; I went to visit his room the other day, and everything was missing. He's just... gone.

My friends try to help, but they don't understand. Buffy is high on her budding cheese-based flirtation with Riley, and Xander and Anya have... whatever they have, and while there's a part of me that is happy for them, that part sits in the back of my brain while this other Willow—a Willow who is bitter and sad and ripped in half—drinks too much and lashes out at everyone.

They all keep saying to give it time. But what they don't understand is that right now, it feels like I don't have time. It feels like this is going to kill me.

Given that my emotions are all over the place, I'm not going to do a love spell. I found a "will-enacting" spell in <u>Witchcraft</u> that I can adapt for my purposes. I don't want it to be indefinite—I've tweaked the ingredients and have designed an exit incantation, so I'll just say, "It is my will that my heart be healed," and then poof! I'll be back to normal again, and everyone will stop looking at me like I'm about to go off the deep end.

A SPELL
TO ENACT ONE'S WILL
(Adapted from DeLauren's Witchcraft)

TOOLS AND INGREDIENTS:

- LARGE WOODEN PENTACLE
- CHALICE FILLED WITH BOILING WATER
- RED CANDLES (20)
- OFFERING PLATES (3)
- APPLE SEEDS
- RED SANDALWOOD POWDER
- DRIED LEAVES (preferably yellow, to represent persuasion; perhaps honey locust)
- MILKSTONE

DIRECTIONS:

This spell is all about balancing the elements. Find a place where you are surrounded by water, then create a circle from your twenty red candles, large enough that you can sit at its center with three offering plates and the pentacle before you. The plate to your left should hold the apple seeds (to represent potential life, or beginnings), the plate in front of you should contain the red sandalwood powder (to represent the present), and put the dried honey locust leaves in the plate to your right (to represent death, or the future).

After lighting the candles, take your position at the circle's center. Add the milkstone to the chalice of boiling water. It will dissolve and form a milky liquid. Starting with the apple seeds, and moving from left to right (life to death), gather a small bit of each ingredient in your hands. Crushing them within your fists, say the following:

> **HARKEN WELL, YE ELEMENTS.**
>
> **I SUMMON THEE NOW.**

Sprinkle the mixture in your hands at the four lower points of the pentacle (representing air, water, earth, and fire) while saying:

> **CONTROL THE OUTSIDE, CONTROL WITHIN**
>
> **LAND AND SEA, FIRE AND WIND**
>
> **OUT OF MY PASSIONS, A WEB BE SPUN**
>
> **FROM THIS EVEN' FORTH, MY WILL BE DONE**
>
> **SO MOTE IT BE.**

Pour the smoking contents of the chalice over the pentacle, finishing at the top point, which represents spirit.

From this point forward, the world should conform to your stated intentions. When you are ready for the spell to be over, say:

> **LET THE HEALING POWER BEGIN.**
>
> **LET MY WILL BE SAFE AGAIN.**
>
> **AS THESE WORDS OF PEACE ARE SPOKEN,**
>
> **LET THIS HARMFUL SPELL BE BROKEN.**

ha! So you knew there was a [po]tential for badness! —X

[T]here was potential for funny [t]oo. Remember the funny? —W

BUFFY AND SPIKE'S WEDDING

THE BRONZE

INVITATION (tentative)

Joyce and Hank Summers (and Rupert Giles?) cordially invite you to celebrate the marriage of their daughter

Buffy Anne Summers

to

William the Bloody

at a TBD location free of crucifixes or holy water

(but not at an actual graveyard or crypt)

sometime after dusk

on the evening of February 12, 2000

Buffy, I'm touched. Never in a million years would I have attended or paid a penny for this, but I am touched. —G

Will . . . I thought you said you burned all of this. —B

I tried. I did. But . . . I mean, look at it. Can you think of any better reminder as to why spells like this are a no-no? Also, sometimes, when Tara or I were feeling cranky, we'd go, "Do you need to look at Buffy's plans for marrying Spike again?" And we'd pull it out, and we'd laugh, and suddenly nothing seemed so . . .
    Sorry. —W

I hate you. —B

Come on, Buff. It's not so bad. You could have been, oh, I don't know, running from a buttload's worth of crazy because someone said you were a demon magnet. —X

You ARE a demon magnet, Xander. But Buffy—one thwarted bride to another, let's talk about this seating chart. Your guests will have nothing to talk about if you don't intermingle the supernatural and the human. Bridal magazines are very clear about having a mix of new and familiar faces at each table. —A

She has a point. And look, I know we're not under this particular mumbo jumbo anymore, but I need to make something clear: Angel is still not invited. —G

Oh, but we'd invite Drusilla? —B

You can be damn well sure that if I'm getting hitched, she's invited so I can rub her bloody face in it. —G

Consider this my request to be blind again, please. Or illiterate. —G

IF THIS EVER HAPPENS FOR REAL, I SO CALL DIBS ON BEST MAN. —ANDREW

Who gave the book to Andrew? I specifically said no one give the book to Andrew. —B

He seemed bored. And he does kind of magick, so maybe he could help. —D

He's EVIL, Dawn!!!!! —B

Formerly evil. And so is the groom!!!! —D

SEATING CHART

TABLE ONE
(Wedding Party)

Buffy (bride)

Spike (groom)

Willow (maid of honor?)

Xander (cool guyfriend of honor?)

Mom

Giles

Dad (maybe; talk with Mom)

TABLE THREE

Drusilla

Willy

Darla

That vampire who was in the cell next to me at the Initiative

Clem

Those Fyarl demons who used to work for me

Teeth, the loan shark

Spike, I've never met half these people. —B

That's because you'd slay them, pet. We wouldn't have to feed them. They'll all eat someone before the reception. —S

TABLE TWO

Angel

Cordelia

Wesley

Riley (?)

Oz (maybe; talk to Willow)

ON COMBINING MAGICKAL ENERGIES

December 15, 1999

Blessed freakin' be—there is another witch in my Wicca group. Her name is Tara, and she started coming a few weeks ago. She never said much, so I didn't realize that she had actual power until things got a little life-and-death the other night when the Hellmouth coughed up its latest monsters of the week, the Gentlemen. They came to town, stole everyone's voices, and tried to take seven hearts, but Buffy was able to make their heads explode. Before she did, however, they managed to corner Tara and me in Stevenson.

I thought we were goners. There I was, cowering on the floor of the laundry room with a sprained ankle, desperately trying to move a vending machine when I haven't been able to move anything heavier than a pencil despite working at it for months. Suddenly, I felt her fingers thread through my own, followed by a rush of warmth that I can only describe as light traveling through her palm and into mine. When I looked at the vending machine again, I not only knew it would move, I felt the power push out from my body. No spell I did with Amy ever felt like that.

Tara says that she's been practicing magick ever since she was little, and yet she acts like I am the powerful, advanced one. (It probably helps that she wasn't around for last week's "Hey, you're blind! Hey, you're imperiled! Hey, you're engaged to your mortal enemy!" magickal rock bottom. I'm starting to run out of recipes for guilt cookies. I should also probably ditch the talisman that D'Hoffryn gave me for wreaking so much havoc, right? I mean, I don't ever want to be a vengeance demon.)

Tara's coming over today after classes to work on some exercises for channeling and sharing energy. My books say that the more two witch buddies practice together, the easier it will be to borrow each other's power and to draw power from the things around me.

For the first time since Oz left, it feels like there's something to look forward to.

CHAKRAS

CROWN CHAKRA

This is found at the top of the head, and is our ultimate spiritual door, a portal to magickal wisdom and a greater understanding of the universe. It's white.

You can go ahead and call this the Xander chakra. I accept. —X

You are pasty white. —A

THIRD EYE CHAKRA

This chakra is situated in the middle of the forehead, just above the eyebrows. It's the seat of psychic, clairvoyant energy and is associated with indigo (or violet).

THROAT CHAKRA

This has to do with communication, in both the physical and spiritual worlds. Oz was clearly missing this chakra. Represented by the color blue.

HEART CHAKRA

This is the source of one's ability to give and receive love. Sometimes, for your own sanity, you have to put a big old closed sign on it. It's got a green thing going on, which doesn't really make sense to me, but okay.

Love = money, money = green. Please explain your confusion. —A

SOLAR PLEXIS CHAKRA

This is the seat of the will. It helps you make decisions and carry out your ambitions. In other words, it's the Buffy chakra. It's even ~~blond~~ yellow.

SACRAL CHAKRA

Situated just below the navel, this is the center of sexuality, sensuality, and emotions, and is associated with the color orange. We'll just call it the snuggle chakra.

ROOT CHAKRA

Located at the base of the spine near the tailbone, it's associated with physical needs like food, sleep, shelter, and mochas. Represented by the color red.

SIMPLE CONE OF POWER

In a room purified with incense, sit across from a fellow practitioner, legs crossed. Decide what kind of energy you are looking to build, and focus on the part of the body that corresponds with that chakra.

Close your eyes, join hands, and visualize the energy as it spirals above you, narrowing to a point over your heads. This represents the concentration, or "cone," of your joined power. It may help to picture the energy as different colors, depending on which spell you hope to perform.

TEST FOR SYNCHRONICITY
(OR, A SPELL TO WEAPONIZE ROSES)

This is a spell to ensure that you are in tune with your magickal partner before attempting anything big.

TOOLS AND INGREDIENTS:

- SALT
- STEMMED ROSE (not fully in bloom)

DIRECTIONS:

Draw the symbol for air in salt and place the rose in the middle. The two practitioners should take seats on opposite sides so that their hands join over the symbol.

Concentrate on building energy from the heart chakra, visualizing it rising into the air. Once the rose is floating, work together to pluck off its petals one by one.

(So, this one maybe got away from us a little bit when the rose sort of zipped around the room and combusted. But like Tara said, at least we got the petals off! . . . I think my heart chakra might still be a little rusty.)

February 8, 2000

Here's an interesting development—Riley, our mild-mannered Psychology TA and supposedly normal Buffy dater, has turned out to be one of the commando guys that we've seen lurking about and zapping demons and vampires. Gotta say, Buffy's ability to romantically home in on the weirdo fish in the Sunnydale sea remains on point.

> Hey, what about . . . never mind.
> —B

According to Riley the commando guys are part of an organization called the Initiative, which is headed by none other than Professor Walsh—I don't know if this makes me more or less accepting of the fact that we're still waiting to get our midterm papers back. They've been enthusiastic about bringing Buffy aboard their operation, but I still think we should be a little wary. You know that I'm usually the first girl in line to go "Yay, science!" but there's something very take-no-prisoners about their attitude that rubs me the wrong way.

Look at Spike. They put a chip in his head, and now he can't bite anyone, not even if they are wearing their most attractive paisley blouse and are having a very good hair day. I'm not saying it's not a good thing that he can't attack humans, but what was the point? Why not just kill him? There's something we're not being told.

I'm about to go over to Giles's apartment. Apparently the Initiative shot Spike with a tracker and are on their way to collect. If I can do a spell to disrupt the signal, it will buy us more time to figure out which side we should be fighting on.

(Funny thing about this spell—you'd think it was designed with beacon interference in mind, but it actually dates from the late nineteenth century. This guy just really hated Edison. Witches are kind of a Luddite-y bunch . . . which I should have guessed from looking at Giles, but still.)

> Please, Willow. I do use light bulbs. I just don't think they should be spiral. —G

A Spell to Ionize the Air
(Adapted from DeLauren's Witchcraft)

TOOLS AND INGREDIENTS:

- DOLL'S EYE CRYSTAL*

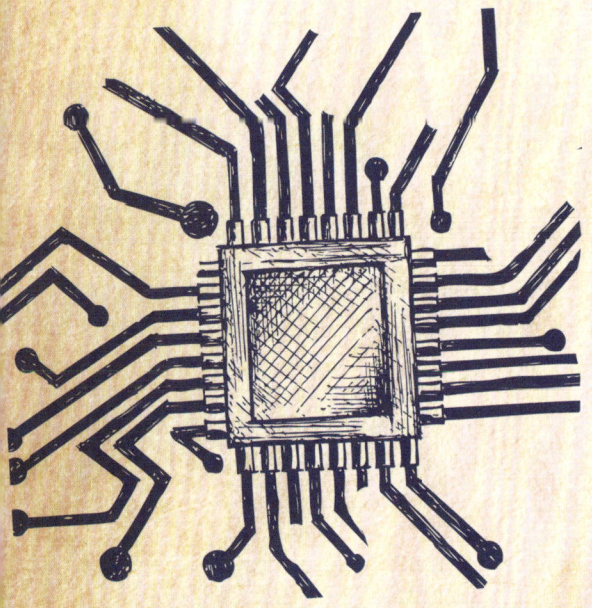

> *A gift from Tara! These crystals are supposed to magnify a witch's power by three. I've been looking for one of these forever, and she, being the sweet Wicca goddess lady she is, just gave it to me. I have to figure out something to give her in return.
>
> —Willow

DIRECTIONS:

Hold a crystal in the palm of your hand and use it as the prism through which to focus your energy. Say the following incantation:

Tropo, Strato, Meso, Aero, Iona, Exo.

Elements are brought to bear.

Wind, earth, and water churn amidst the fire.

Let the air be burned!

Not my best look
—W

February 15, 2000

I hate to say I told you so, but I was right about there being something off with the Initiative. Professor Walsh tried to have Buffy killed because she was getting too close to discovering that the good professor has been cobbling together demon parts to create a super-soldier, which—of course—ended up becoming a super-monster. Then, this morning, we learned that the monster—Adam—turned around and killed her.

This means that not only is it time to move past getting a grade back on that midterm paper—it's time to figure out how to pull on my big-witch pants. Not just for the usual "being a hero" reasons, but also because I don't think we will all survive spending another night hiding in Xander's basement. It is a hellish pit of despair, and I live in a dorm room with a pet rat who used to be a person.

Last night, while lying awake on my one third of Xander's so-called sofa bed and listening to Anya snore, Giles squeak around on his beach ball, and Buffy mutter about "muffin people" (really crossing my fingers that that one's not a prophecy), I started thinking of all the spells that Tara and I had been doing, and all the doors that have opened since she started helping me figure out my powers. For a long time, I've been thinking about how convenient it would be to have a spell that showed us where in Sunnydale the demons were hanging out so Buffy could save time on patrolling. And then, voilà! It suddenly unfurled in my head like a map I had forgotten was in the glove box.

I need Tara's help with it, though, and since she hasn't gotten back to me yet, I think I'll just head over to her room and see if I can catch her. I want to talk to her anyway—even though she acted like it was no big deal (she always acts like things are no big deal), I should have invited her to the Bronze the other night. I need to introduce her to the gang. It's just . . . hard to explain. When I'm hanging out with her, I feel so calm and at peace, and yet kind of nervous at the same time. She's helped me so much—with magick, with getting over Oz leaving—that I kind of want to protect her from all the crazy that comes from being friends with the Slayer.

> Oh, there were many rats down there. It's possible one of them was also a former person. I called him Clyde—he always watched as I got dressed. —A

> You're forgetting the endearing sense of whimsy and the "I'll Punch Anyone in the Face for Free" card that comes with being the Slayer's friend. —B

A Spell to Locate Demonic Activity in Sunnydale

Tools and Ingredients:

- Mortar and Pestle
- Cotton String
- White Candles (3)
- Sacred Sand
- Brimstone Powder
- Demon Scales

Directions:

Form a square with the cotton string; the area in the square you create represents a map of the land you would like to scan for demonic activity (in this case, Sunnydale). Anchor the "map" with your four crystals, with milky quartz representing the northwest, red quartz the northeast, clear quartz the southeast, and smoky quartz the southwest.

Light all four candles, and place them on a pedestal near where you are sitting, with the dragon wax candle nearest to you. Divide the sand into two parts. Grind one half with the demon scales, the other with the brimstone powder. Have each practitioner choose a mixture and take a pinch in hand.

With closed eyes, one speaker begins:

> Thespia, we walk in shadow,
>
> Walk in blindness.
>
> You are the protector of the night.

The other, eyes also closed, continues:

> Thespia, goddess, ruler of all darkness,
>
> We implore you.
>
> Open a window to the word of the underbeing.

Have both spellcasters blow the dust in their hands across the magickal square outlined by the string, then finish the incantation together.

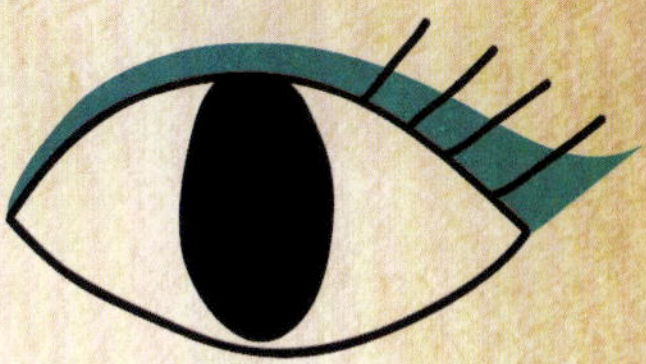

> **With your knowledge,**
> **May we go in safety.**
> **With your grace,**
> **May we speak of your benevolence.**

Open your eyes. Points of demonic activity should be illuminated by various shades of light.

Note: It didn't work! Tara was cool about it—and she let me stay and look at her mom's Book of Shadows afterward—but still. It's embarrassing. I guess Tara's right: We're not ready to call on Thespia yet.

Sexy. Clearly not as sexy as when we did it, Willow, but a close second.
—A

THESPIA (ALSO THESPEIA)

Said to have been the daughter of a water nymph and the river god Asopos, she protected the well after which the Greek city of Thespiae was named. Thespiae was often under attack by monstrous serpents and other scaly ilk, and so she's a good lady to call on when it comes to spells that involve going mano a mano—or magicko a magicko—against the supernatural.
—Willow

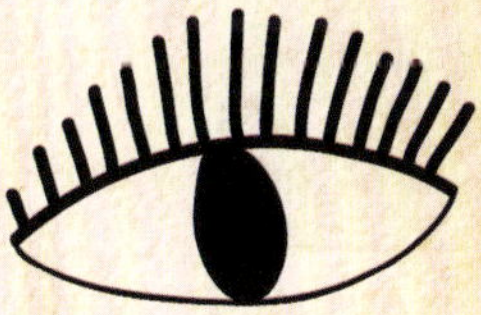

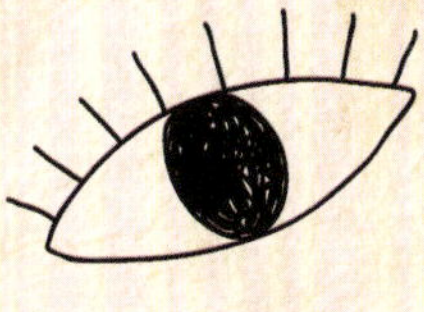

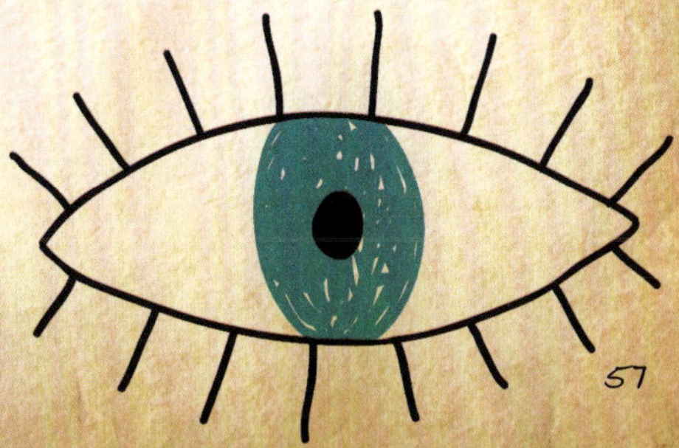

February 29, 2000

I finally did it: I introduced Tara to Buffy. I wasn't planning on it—my intention had been to start with baby steps and take Tara to the Bronze on a low-key night. You know, just a normal friendly outing. An outing for friends who sometimes hold hands . . . I think it was a date. It was a date. It was a date with a girl, and I don't know how I feel about that so I'm just gonna whoosh right on past it at very high speeds and get to the spell part.

Because as it turns out, I don't think I actually introduced Tara to Buffy. For one thing, Buffy's outfit was rivaling Vampire Me's in the I Love Leather department. And two, she was kind of a bitch—as in raging. Tara said that Buffy's energy was off, grating and fragmented when there should be a kind of flow, and suggested that we try an astral projection spell to see what kind of thing might be possessing or affecting her.

It worked. I saw an image of Buffy only she was surrounded by an eerie green light that kept making her flicker in and out. She opened her mouth to speak, but instead of words, only fire came out.

When I opened my eyes, Tara was leaning over me, her hair brushing my cheeks, and for a second I forgot where we were, what we were doing. She asked me what I had seen, and when I told her, she leapt up and grabbed a book off the shelf. She thinks it was done via a Draconian Katra spell, which can imbue an item with the power to let the holder switch bodies with another by clasping hands. It has to be Faith, and it has to have happened the other night.

It's not difficult to conjure. We just need to go to the magic shop in the morning and get a few ingredients . . .

Oh God. I think Tara's my girlfriend.

A Spell to Journey into the Netherworld

(Or, how to use astral projection to see if your friend is really your enemy, or just having a super cranky day)

Tools and Ingredients:

- Clay bowl
- Clay bottle
- Jasmine oil

Directions:

In this spell, one practitioner will be the traveler, the other the anchor. The anchor should pour the jasmine oil from an earthen container into an earthen bowl, then anoint the traveler on the forehead, lips, collarbone, and other touchpoints of the chakras. The traveler repeats the process on the anchor, thus strengthening the bonds between them.

Each practitioner should sit in a way that allows their hips to touch the other's, but with their bodies facing in opposite directions. With your left arm, trace an arc back and forth in the air as though running your fingers through water or sand, while softly chanting:

> **The Inward Eye, the Sightless Sea**
>
> **Ayala flows through the river in me**

Repeat until you begin to feel a channel of light flow from your fingertips. Clasp hands with the stationary arms and hold them up, palm to palm, between your bodies. As the energy begins to rise, the traveler will be seized by a vision.

Draconian Katra Spell
(A Spell to Transfer Spiritual Energies)

Tools and Ingredients:

- Dragon's Blood Oil
- Metal Bowl
- White Candle
- Black Candle
- Red Thread (an arm's length)

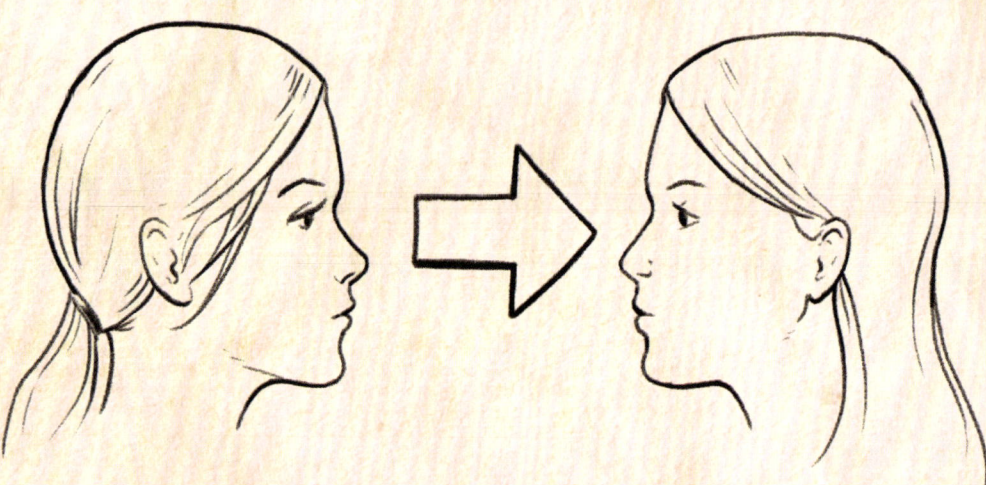

Directions:

Place a metal bowl between two lit candles, one white and one black. Fill with oil of dragon's blood and set aflame. While the fire burns, take your thread and begin to make a knot at one end while visualizing the physical body of a spirit that will be involved in the transfer. While you work, say:

> **Ananta Sesha, your infinite qualities bestow**
>
> **Earth above, air below**

After tying the first knot, move to the other end of the thread and make another, this time focusing on the other person's physical form.

> **From the thousand heads, we ask just two**
>
> **Your penance grants us life anew**

Cast the knotted thread into the fire. A ball of green light should emerge. When clasped between opposing skin, it will transfer the energies between the two human vessels.

MAGIC BOX

April 4, 2000

Something very odd has occurred, and I feel the need to put pen to paper as a way of sorting it all out. Buffy is claiming that Jonathan Levinson—the twentieth century's one true Renaissance Man—is not the kindhearted wunderkind that we all know and love, and is instead something that has us living in an alternate universe of his design.

I admit, based on the mark he bears on his shoulder and the spell that Willow found while flipping through the books Jonathan generously donated to us from his world-renowned collection, there is evidence that some magick could be at play.

I remember the first day he walked into my library. As he approached the circulation desk, I was struck by seeing such an air of self-assurance in someone so young. "This is an old soul," I thought, and I felt inspired to present <u>The Slayer Handbook</u> to him.

"Dear Watcher," he said, with characteristic gentleness. "I am honored that you think me worthy of such a birthright. But I believe you are looking for someone blonder. More female. It has been a while since I've spoken with Quentin at the Council," he added, "but I sense that her name rhymes with Muffy."

"Quite right," I said, and gave a nervous chuckle; what a faux pas to have committed on my first day on the job! Of course he wasn't the slayer. That would turn out to be Buffy, whose idiosyncrasies certainly grew on me, even if we never had the same instant connection. It would be Jonathan who was there with me when I discovered that Buffy would fight the Master and die. It was Jonathan who came to prevent me from taking my vengeance against Angelus, pleading with me to stay alive because he couldn't continue this fight alone.

But it is one of my duties as a Watcher to go beyond my own personal feelings, so I am recording this spell, perhaps as a way of convincing myself that it could not be true.

—Giles

Your One-Stop Spot to Shop for ALL Your Occult Needs

Willow, of all the magick I've done over the course of our acquaintance, is this really the only thing that you decided merited inclusion in this book? Much like the Jonathan Levinson swimsuit calendar that I found in my possession, this moment in time is something that I would very much like to forget. —G

Xander used that calendar for the rest of the year. —A

So happy to hear that I grew on you, Giles. Like mold, or a fungus. I'm touched. Really. —B

God the soaps. Give us more of this. —G

Wasn't in love with my tomb, though. —G

Yes, Spike, we all heard you laughing in the basement. May I remind you that in this alternate universe, you spent your entire life lurking behind a tomb. —G

MAGIC BOX

THE SPELL OF THE PARAGON
(A Spell that Transforms Its Caster into a Sort of Ideal Man, the Best of Everything... But at a Grave Cost)

TOOLS AND INGREDIENTS:

- WILLOW BARK
- SKIN OF CORAL SNAKE
- SKIN OF KING SNAKE
- PEACH
- BEANS OF CASTOR

A brand in the shape of the symbol of the Paragon. The triangle shall be made of lead, the spokes of silver.

DIRECTIONS:

The ingredients of this spell have both light and dark energies within them. The caster must take great care to separate them.

Crush the castor beans and strain out the oil (beneficial) while retaining the rinds (harmful).

Remove the flesh of the peach (beneficial) and reserve the stone (harmful).

Fill the king snake skin with the nonpoisonous items, while the skin of the coral snake should be filled with the poisonous leftovers.

Build a fire using willow bark, then burn both snake skins and their contents in it. The resulting flames should be used to heat the brand that you will use to mark the caster's body.

(Note: The act of bringing good into the world will create a resulting force of evil, usually in the form of a monster. Perhaps that monster came in the form of the sequel to Jonathan's best-selling autobiography, <u>Short in Stature, Tall in Everything Else</u>, which I felt really did not live up to its predecessor...)

Your One-Stop Spot to Shop for ALL Your Occult Needs

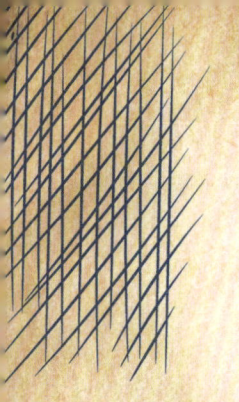
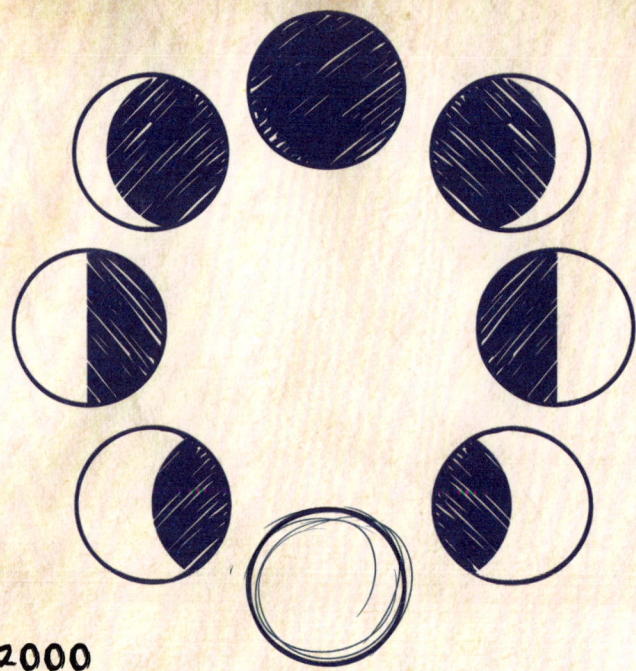

May 2, 2000

Oz came back. There we were, having an uneventful meeting in Giles's apartment—Anya being difficult for the sake of being Anya, me basking in the fact that I've brought Tara and no one is acting like it's a thing—and suddenly, boom. Door opens. Enter the ex-boyfriend.

Tara left before I could stop her. I didn't know what to say to her. I didn't even really know what to say to Oz when he came to my dorm room later. We talked all night, just like we used to, but I wasn't able figure out how to tell him that I might have feelings for someone else. After he left, I decided that I had to tell someone, and in the face of Buffy's innocent, rah-rah "Your prodigal boyfriend is back" speech, it was easy to say no, it's complicated because of Tara.

She tried to be supportive, but I could tell that I had thrown her for a loop. I still kind of feel like I'm on that loop, too. Oz is not the Oz who left, but I am also not the same Willow. It's easy to slip back into her skin when we're talking or when he touches me, but the longer I wear it, the more I feel it start to pinch.

At some point during our midnight talk, I changed the subject by telling him that I had been keeping this book as a record of the spells that I've done and have been learning. He showed me the Moleskine that he used on his travels; it made me smile to see that he had a habit of shoving pages in every which way, a lot like me. I asked if I could have something from it, and he tore out the page on how he first learned to resist transformation during the full moon, saying that he didn't need it anymore.

After he left, I tried the chant on the torn-out page. It didn't work. I have no inner cool. Because deep inside, I know the truth—no matter what happens, or what it means for my family and friends, I want to be with Tara. I want to be with Tara.

A Technique to Keep Your Inner Cool

(For Werewolves. Doesn't Work So Well for Willows.)

February 9, 2000

Found some monks in Tibet. It turns out that they really like Radiohead, which makes sense when you think about it, but also doesn't. They don't talk much, so I am working on being less chatty.

One of their members is a werewolf, but he doesn't wolf out unless he wants to. He's been teaching me, helping me carve beads out of mountain ash that I'll keep with me on every full moon.

As I carve them, I meditate. It feels a lot like shop class, only on a mountain and with more gongs.

I miss Willow.

I think of her as I carve. I am supposed to think of things that keep me human and say:

"I am calm. I am rooted. I am calm. I am rooted."

When I am done, I will string the beads on a line, like a rosary, and carry them in my pocket, along with a monkshood flower.

The new moon is in a few days.

And then we'll see if I can go back.

With You, Always

May 16, 2000

I wish I could say that letting everyone know I was with Tara went perfectly, but it didn't. Not because of my friends, but because of a bleached-blond doo-doo head who should have gotten staked a long time ago.

I should have known better than to trust anything that Spike says. That's the thing about friendships, though. You think they are strong and rock-solid and then someone sweeps in and preys on your deepest fears, and suddenly you are at each other's throats and Giles is drunk upstairs.

But it's okay. Buffy figured out that Spike was working with Adam, and that his whispering in our respective ears was just a ploy to keep us all apart so that Adam could corner Buffy alone. That big old monster doesn't know what's about to hit him—Xander, Giles, and I think we've figured out a spell that we can use to beat him.

Giles says that the Enjoining Spell was created as a way to imbue a Slayer with the powers of her ancestors, particularly the First Slayer—but he thinks that there's a way to tweak it so that we can get imbue-y with other attributes as well—_our_ attributes. If we can all get into the Initiative base, we should able to make it so that Buffy faces Adam as a large-hearted, magic-having, Sumerian-speaking super-Slayer.

Why nothing from me on the Enjoining Ritual, for instance? I was part of this. I clearly remember jotting down several notes, any of which I would have donated to your recording efforts. Not to mention that I'm the one who brought the bloody magic gourd.—G

The Enjoining Ritual

Directions:

Place the blessed gourd in the center of your casting room and surround it with four evenly spaced, already lit candles. Have the three whose spirits will be poured into the fourth vessel sit around it. Have one of the supplicants begin the incantation:

Tools and Ingredients:

- Gourd that has been blessed by magick and carved with the symbols of convergence and unity
- Candles (4, any color)
- Tarot cards (one for each spirit that will be combined within the vessel)

    The Hermit – Giles   The Knight of Swords – Xander
    The High Priestess – Willow   The Hand – Buffy

> The power of the Slayer and all who wield it.
> Last to ancient first, we invoke thee.
> Grant us thy domain and primal strength.
> Accept us and the power we possess.
> Make us mind and heart and spirit enjoined
> Let the hand encompass us. Do thy will.

Take the four tarot cards, and hand them to those in the circle. Have each supplicant place their card in front of the gourd while saying their corresponding quality.

> Spiritus . . . spirit
>
> Animus . . . heart
>
> Sophus . . . mind

Finally, the initial speaker should place the card of the vessel in the gourd.

> And Manus . . . the hand.

Finish the incantation together:

> We enjoin that we may inhabit the vessel, the hand.
> Daughter of Sineya, First of the Ones,
> We implore thee: Admit us.
> Bring us to the vessel! Take us now!
> We are heart. We are mind.

SOPHUS

ANIMUS

MANUS

SUPER-SLAYER SUMERIAN SPELLS

Willow asked me to write down exactly what kind of magick the super-Slayer version of me used in my fight with Adam, and since I'm carefree Big-Badless girl these days, I was like "Pfft! No problem." After all, it's not every day that Chosen One responsibilities involve no-nonsense paperwork. It's kind of refreshing, actually.

Anyway, there I was, in the heart of the Initiative, facing down Adam and—I don't want to say that I was losing, exactly, but it wouldn't be inaccurate to say that I was . . . left of winning. I had broken the skewer thing that he was so fond of popping out of his arm, but all that did was encourage him to show off his new arm, which was all machine gun-y. I ducked behind a control center to escape the hail of bullets, and when I came up, everything was different. I felt strong. And not just physically strong—it was like I had eyes everywhere, like I knew exactly what to do and how to do it.

He hit me with another hail of bullets, but I said something jazzy like:

> SHA ME-EN-DAN. GESH-TOOG
> ME-EN-DAN. ZEE ME-EN-DEN.
> OO-KHUSH-TA ME-OOL-LEE-A
> BA-AB-TUM-MU-DO-EN.

I waved my hand, and the bullets fell down at my feet. He tried a rocket launcher next, but I said "Kur!" and it turned into a bird. Then I did a little wax-on, wax-off action, and his gun retracted into his arm.

This time when I went up to fight him, it was like he couldn't touch me. I grabbed his wrists and then punched him in the face—Pow! Pow! Pow! Then I leaned backed and kicked him in the chest—Bam!—and he went flying. He was like "How can you . . . ?" and I was like "You can never hope to grasp the source of our power." Then I flung him into a wall, reached into his chest, grabbed the uranium battery, and said, "But yours is right here."

It was very Mortal Kombat—only Mortal Kombat with a character who has really good hair.

Of course, after it was over, the Rasta-mama First Slayer kind of stalked us all through our dreams, so it's definitely going to be one for the "use sparingly" file.

MAGIC

For the record, please let it be known that I did not tell Buffy to write this on the back of her Psychology final. —Willow

Like I was going to get a passing grade in this class, anyway. The teacher tried to kill me. Literally! —B

Nice finishing line. Points for style. —S

Thank you, Spike. —B

> I've done a little research since Buffy gave me this very... vivid... account, and as far as I can tell, all the spells that she used were variations on an ancient Sumerian Spell of Peaceful Resistance. It calls on Enlil, King of the Gods, who is said to have given mankind all the spells and incantations that the spirits of good and evil must obey.
> —Willow

SEPTEMBER 26, 2000

Things have been pretty slow in Sunnydale since we defeated Adam. Wait! Dracula—yes, the real, not-quite-living-but-super-dreamy Dracula—showed up and put Xander and Buffy in his thrall! ... Come to think of it, I may need to reevaluate my bar for "pretty slow," as it's possible my perspective has been skewed by four years of dealing with the Hellmouth. I don't have a philosophy class this semester, but I ask: If something happens in Sunnydale and it doesn't involve an apocalypse or a big complicated spell requiring various difficult-to-acquire ingredients, did it ever truly exist?

Buffy's still being a little hard on Dawn for accidentally inviting a vampire into the Summers home, so I've been trying to be extra nice to her these days. It must be hard being kid sister to the Slayer—I've had my fair share of standing in the Buffy shadow—but she's had to grow up with it. I know it bugs Buffy sometimes when I defend Dawn, but I can't help it. I have all this involuntary empathy; she reminds me of myself sometimes, with her weird facts and eagerness to be a part of the gang.

I asked Dawn if she wanted to try to do a spell with me and Tara, but she got all weird and said that she didn't think her mom was all that cool with witchcraft, which is strange, because I always felt like Joyce was very open-minded and supportive. It's probably a good thing though—my magick's back to being kind of fifty-fifty, or at least sixty-forty. I tried yet another spell to turn Amy Rat back into Amy Human, and it didn't work.

Still, I think something happened. Since Hecate hasn't been responding to being asked nicely to leave, I thought maybe we could try banishing her instead, but I forgot that black hellebore can also be used in spells to summon demons and incite aggression ... and since I tried the spell, Amy Rat has been watching me and rubbing her paws together, kind of like she's plotting something.

Tara said that if she starts squeaking about global domination, we should just give her to what remains of the UC Sunnydale Psychology Department and say "Have at it." I know she was joking, but ... let's not rule it out just yet.

> If you like high-maintenance dirt lovers, I guess.—B

> Not to mention that some monks took an ancient ball of energy and turned it into me. But no worries. I realize it would probably tear a philosophical hole in the universe if someone noticed. You didn't think it was strange that I had never shown up in the book until now?—D

> I did think it was strange ... eventually. Can we just chalk this one up to monk magick, Dawnie?—W

> Okay. But try sharing a bathroom with the Buffy shadow. It leaves wet towels everywhere.—D

> At least the Buffy shadow washes the towels every now and then.—B

> Where are you finding all these towels? Ever since the potentials moved in, towels are like black market goods. I used an oven mitt the other day.—A

DE-RATTING SPELL ATTEMPT NUMBER THREE
(OR, A SPELL TO MAKE AN ANIMAL REALLY, REALLY SMART AND MAYBE DIABOLICAL)

DIRECTIONS:

Make a strong infusion of the hellebore by pouring boiling water over the flower and straining out the botanical material.

Let the liquid cool, then sprinkle it on the being you believe is inhabited by magick or spiritual forces while chanting:

> ENYO, WE BESEECH YOU,
>
> TAKE UP ARMS.
>
> GRANT US YOUR WISDOM IN WAR
>
> AND LET THE POWERS THAT INHABIT THIS CREATURE
>
> BE DRIVEN OUT BEFORE THEY HARM.

TOOLS AND INGREDIENTS:
- STRAINER
- BOTTLE OR BOWL
- BLACK HELLEBORE*

*Maybe don't use this again...

October 10, 2000

Giles bought the Magic Box! I <u>am</u> a little worried about him, given Sunnydale's high rate of magic shop ownership-related deaths, but at the same time, it means that pretty soon we'll be rolling in reptile parts!

...That statement created an unexpected visual, and I would like to take it back. Moving on.

The other night a Tothric demon, Toth, came after Buffy—it tried to hit her with something called a Ferula Gemini. If it had hit Buffy, it would have split her into two Buffies—one a purely Slayer Buffy, and the other an easy-to-kill Buffy. But instead of hitting Buffy with the spell, he hit Xander, and now we've had two Xanders running around. One's all fancy-pants, and the other is kind of like, well, Xander if he woke up on the wrong side of a pile of garbage. And I mean that literally.

Ah, memories. I miss that guy. —X

For a while, each Xander thought that the other was a demon, and there was a slight misunderstanding where they tried to kill each other. They've sorted out their differences (I'm not sure if I'm happy about that—two Xanders is one Xander too much), and now we're getting ready to do a spell to put them back together. To be honest, with this kind of sophisticated demon spell, it's really the initial magick that's doing all the work, so you don't need much more than a simple statement and a moderately talented witch to bring order back into the universe.

However, given the number of my recent spells that have gone a little wonky, I don't know that I'm going to be super forthright about how easy this one is. I could use a mark in the "I Did a Spell and None of My Friends Suffered Terribly!" column. I told Giles to draw a pentagram on the floor in chalk and light some candles, but I'm pretty sure we wouldn't have even needed to do that. Still, it's important to maintain an illusion—just now I told him that he shouldn't be afraid to crouch down on the floor and really get into it. I might also tell the Xanders that they need to do the Snoopy Dance just to, you know, "complete the ritual."

I suspected as much. And I'll have you know it took an hour to mop that off the floor. —G

REVERSING DEMONIC SPELLS
(OR, A SPELL TO POP TWO XANDERS BACK TOGETHER)

TOOLS AND INGREDIENTS:
- CHALK
- ESSENCE OF SLUG CANDLES (3)
  (He's going to have to get rid of them somehow. Not sure why Giles decided to stock those.)

  > Are you kidding? We got them at 25 percent of cost from the distributor. Tell people something's an aphrodisiac and it's like a license to print money. But not a real license. I already made that mistake. —A

DIRECTIONS:
Make a big show of needing to draw a large pentacle on the floor and place candles in three of its points. Make both Xanders stand within the pentacle's confines.

Say:

LET THIS SPELL BE ENDED.

Yep. That's really it.

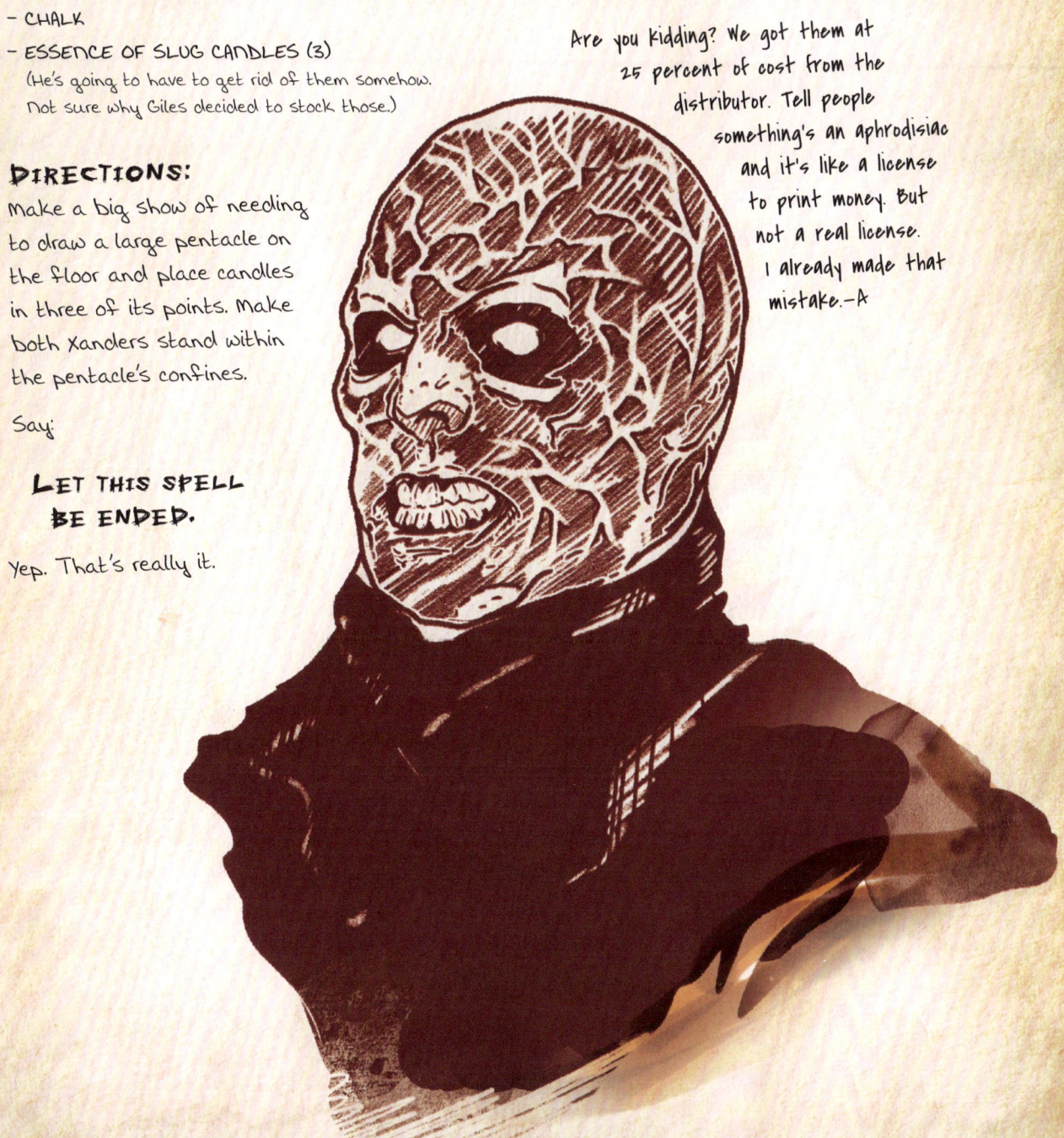

OCTOBER 24, 2000

Buffy's been having a hard time lately. First, Joyce collapsed and ended up in the hospital, and then Riley found out that his stint as Professor Walsh's experiment was harming his heart. They're both doing okay now, but she's become convinced that what's affecting Joyce is otherworldly in nature after the doctors at Sunnydale General shared that their medical consensus is a big case of "I dunno, let's do more tests."

I'm not sure what to think. Buffy did find a strange glowy ball thing the other day on patrol, but this is also Sunnydale, where the secret town motto is "Don't Trip Over a Corpse or Supernatural Object on Your Way Out." She says that the security guard where it was found showed up at the hospital, suddenly crazy, and I can tell from her Determined Buffy Face that she's not going to rest until otherworldly explanations are ruled out.

Anya suggested that Buffy use Cloutier's spell to sense supernatural influence, and it's not the worst idea that she's ever come up with (although let's be honest—it's a low bar). I've been studying Cloutier's work for a while, and despite some weird sixteenth-century norms (that are not, nor should they ever have been, normal), he really knew his stuff.

The thing is—trancework can be pretty advanced. I know that Buffy's started training with Giles again, but a spelled trance still demands an intense amount of focus. With that in mind, I've tweaked the kinds of incense it uses to aid in concentration and add a little bit of beginner's luck.

Hey! Don't forget I'm the one who came up with the way to fight Glory . . . although I still think we could have worked a piano in somewhere. That always seems to work on the unkillable villains. Maybe for the First.—A

CLOUTIER'S TRANCE
(A SPELL TO SEE SPELLS)

TOOLS AND INGREDIENTS:

– OIL OF ABRAMELIN
– RED SAND
– VIOLET INCENSE
(for increased luck)

ACACIA INCENSE (for increased psychic powers)

CARDAMOM INCENSE (for increased concentration)

PURPLE TAPERED CANDLE
(the taller the better)

DIRECTIONS:

Place a dot of the Abramelin on your third eye; this will help protect you against any spirits you might find on your journey. Light the three incenses and let their scents mingle in the air.

Create a meditation circle using the red sand, and take your position at its center. With your eyes closed, visualize a curtain. Picture yourself reaching out to the curtain and drawing it back. Repeat until you pull back the curtain to reveal a beckoning figure. Open your eyes. Any magick or demonic influence that has been influencing or altering your existence or the existence of those around you will be revealed.

THE BRONZE

Snagged this from Anya's binder at the Magic Shop. It's not every day you meet someone versed in the lost art of Sobekian magick. The one book I have on the subject glosses over the actual spell parts. —Willow

SOBEKIAN BLOODSTONE MAGICK

THE NO-SELL LIST

Since I've been informed that calling one's boss an idiot is not a workplace-appropriate way to address things that concern me, I've decided to start compiling a list of items that should not be sold together here at the Magic Box, no matter what, just in case anyone else feels like being a dummy and wants to sell highly dangerous magick to ancient, all-powerful beings in search of a Key. I've used helpful pictographs, as, given the stupidity that's already been displayed, it's obvious one can't be too careful. —Anya

ITEMS:

KHUL'S AMULET + SOBEKIAN BLOODSTONE = :(

Anyone buying these two things together can only be interested in doing a spell like Glory did, one that takes a cute little snake and turns it into a spawn of Sobek for their own purposes. That person is also probably bad news; the Temple of Sobek's initiation rituals alone could give you a rap sheet a mile long. Longer in Alabama.

DIRECTIONS:

Put the reptile you wish to transform in a clay vessel. Begin the Arabic chant, but before you begin the last line ("Come into being . . ."), hold Khul's amulet above the vessel.

TOOLS AND INGREDIENTS:

- Sobekian bloodstone
- Khul's amulet
- Clay pot
- A reptile (preferably poisonous, and of the genus that matches the bloodstone you are using)

ARABIC:

النموذج السفيني، أصدرت جديدة.

وإذا ما توفرت الإرادة، للدخول لنا الرجال.

النموذج السفيني، أصدرت جديدة.

القاعدة هي حجر، واستحم في الدم.

جوهره هو النار والعناصر مخلخل

تأتي إلى حيز الوجود وتنشأ!

TRANSLATION:

SOBEK, GRANT THE POWER, THAT IT MAY MOLD THIS WRETCHED CREATURE, THAT IT MAY BE REBORN, THAT IT MAY SERVE WITH BLOODSTONE, WITH RARE GEM, COME INTO BEING AND ARISE!

ARISE!

JANUARY 9, 2001

Riley left the other day, and he hardly gave Buffy any warning. She's trying to put on Happy Buffy Face, but having been on the same end of a dump-and-ditch, I know that she must be devastated.

Last night, Tara and I tried to come up with ideas to help her keep her mind off of things, but other than watching terrible ice skating movies, Buffy doesn't have many hobbies apart from slaying. So we started thinking about slaying accessories, and ta-da! Simulated sunlight. Maybe if we figure out a way for Buffy to take out vamp nests with magick sunlight, she would have more time to look for the Key, take care of her mom—who seems to be doing well since her surgery!—and watch the aforementioned terrible ice skating movies. Who knows. Maybe she could even find a different kind of favorite movie.

We're going to swing by the Magic Box tomorrow to snag some ingredients and try it out. Giles is in London seeing if the Watchers' Council has any information on Glory, and while he didn't come out and say it, I could tell he was worried about Anya running things alone.

I still can't believe that Buffy and Riley called it quits and yet somehow Xander and Anya are still going strong.

SIMULATED SUNLIGHT SPELL
(A SLAYING ACCESSORY)

TOOLS AND INGREDIENTS:
- FLEABANE* ($0.15)
- BINDWEED ($4.26)
- SALAMANDER EYES ($6.00)
- MORTAR AND PESTLE
- CAULDRON

(*Fleabane is not the most stable of ingredients, so make sure to be all about the e-nun-ci-a-ting.)

($5 if I decide to still give you the 12 for $10 pricing. Given that you destroyed the Magic Box when you went all dark and crazy, I'm thinking not. $6 for you.)

I still maintain that I was trying to help Buffy with this spell, but if you want to charge me extra on my next order, fine. —W

That would be great. Thanks!
I only take cash. No personal checks. —A

DIRECTIONS:
In a room where you are unlikely to have any interruptions, bring your cauldron to a boil. Grind the fleabane, bindweed, and salamander eyes until you have a dark paste. Add the paste to the boiling water, close your eyes, and begin the following incantation:

SPIRITS OF LIGHT, I INVOKE THEE.

LET THE GLOOM OF DARKNESS PART BEFORE YOU.

LET THE MOONLIGHT BE MADE PALE BY YOUR PRESENCE.

SPIRITS OF LIGHT, GRANT MY WISHES.

COALESCE AND TAKE SHAPE.

ENLIGHTEN US ALL.

SPELLS TO FIGHT A TROLL
(WHO HAPPENS TO BE ANYA'S FORMER BOYFRIEND)

JANUARY 10, 2001

So... funny story. You know how I said that fleabane could make the simulated sunlight spell very unstable and you should make sure to enunciate and have no distractions? Well, Anya and I started to argue in the middle of the spell and ended up releasing Olaf, a troll who went a little hammer happy on the Bronze and bone breaky on Xander's wrist.

   I think Anya and I finally came to an understanding, though. While I still think she could use some work when it comes to the whole, you know, being a person thing, I know that her feelings for Xander are genuine and she's finally convinced that my lips are really only for girls now. (Not to mention that seeing her last boyfriend, the troll, gives me a sense of how far she's come.)

   I just wish I knew that we actually sent Olaf to a troll dimension. The spell we found was really more like dimension roulette. I tried to use ingredients to make it more specific, but I think it's just as possible that he ended up somewhere else. Tara told me to stop worrying about it.

A Spell to Take an Opponent's Weapon During Battle

(In this case, a giant troll hammer)

TOOLS AND INGREDIENTS:

- Runic tablets

DIRECTIONS:

Cast a set of nine runes while focusing on the threat that you would like to make benign. If the casting is favorable—look for the appearance of "luck," "strength," "success," "victory" and other similar symbols—continue to the incantation below. If not, try again when circumstances have changed.

Instrumentum ultionis, telum fabuloso,

Surge, surge, terram pro voca.

Vola cum viribus, dominum tuum nega. Vola!

TRANSLATION:

Tool of vengeance, weapon mythic,

Arise, arise, defy the earth.

Fly with force, deny thy master. Fly!

I saw "luck" and "victory" in the casting, and decided to take a chance. There was also "fertility" so let's all just send up a thank you to the Goddess for not inundating us with troll babies.

—Willow

A Spell to Send an Object to Another Dimension
(In this case, a troll)

Tools and Ingredients:
- Alder branches
- Flowers of the hop plant

HIISI FIGURINE

Directions:
Surround the object or person you wish to transport with items that have a special relationship to the dimension that you hope to reach. (In this case, I raided the Magic Box for all the Norse-ish ingredients we could find, and arranged them around his big troll body. We added some hops at the last minute since he seemed to really like beer.) When you feel that your spread has the correct balance of items, say the following, specifying the object you wish to move and asking for aid from an appropriate deity.

> Freyja, with your power,
>
> Take this troll to your bosom,
>
> And a world of your own choosing.
>
> Let the transposition be complete

I still think you should have let me put a crystal in his belly button. —X

Again—not that kind of troll. —W

Here is a list of dimensions you may send me to, should the need ever arise or if it seems like I just need a vacation.
- Dimension where none of your dates want to eat you
- Dimension where surfaces are always level
- Swimsuit calendar dimension
- Freyja's bosom dimension

—Xander

I'm sensing a theme . . .

a juvenile, pervy theme. —B

Spells to Fight a Hellgod

February 6, 2001

Dawn is the Key, the thing that Glory has been hunting. Even though Buffy told us everything, I'm still having trouble wrapping my head around how all those memories I have of Dawn—her sneaking around outside Buffy's door and listening in whenever I would spend the night, her coming over to sit in the corner of my room, writing in her diary while Buffy and I did our math homework and chatted about Angel and Oz—can be fake.

Buffy's worried. Now that we know Glory is a brain-sucking god, not just your average demon, it seems like our normal slay routine isn't going to cut it. I promised her that I'd start working on some extra magicky magick to help in the fight, starting with some tactical spells that will warn us if Glory is nearby... and hopefully help us run away once she is.

EARLY WARNING ALARM
(TO SET AROUND A BUILDING OR DOMICILE)

The aim of this spell is to combine the powers of the banshee with traditional protective magick. It should create a shrieking sound when any creature who wishes death upon those inside the circle steps within the spell's bounds.

TOOLS AND INGREDIENTS:
- BEESWAX CANDLE
- WILLOW BRANCHES (3)
- LINDEN BRANCHES (3)
- GREEN RIBBON
- PINK CORAL (used to protect children)
- MORTAR AND PESTLE

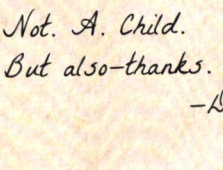

Not. A. Child.
But also—thanks.
        —D

DIRECTIONS:
Grind the pink coral into a fine powder and set aside. Bind the willow and linden branches into a bundle with the green string.

On a night when the moon shines brightly (full or gibbous), light the beeswax candle and call upon the spirit of the banshee ("bean sidhe" in Irish Gaelic) using the following incantation:

> **Bean sidhe, marker of death,**
> **Lend us your voice**
> **So that we may guard our loved ones**
> **And let you rest.**

Use the candle's flame to set fire to the willow and linden branches, then transfer the flaming mess to a larger hearth (or a metal can) where the branches can burn freely. When only smoke remains, gather the ashes.

In front of the building that you would like to protect, pour a semicircle of the ground coral so that it creates a wide arc around the doorway. On the inside and the outside of the semicircle, draw the protection symbols to the left with the ashes of your combined tree branches.

When the last symbol is completed, your protective alarms should be set.

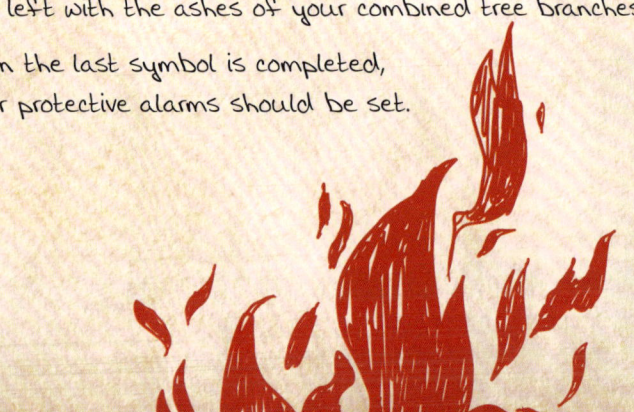

TELEPORTATION SPELL

I've been thinking about the disappearing act that the cash register did when I tried to use Aradia's dust on Olaf the other day; when I got home that night, there the cash register was, just sitting on my bed, all nonchalant-like. I had managed to teleport it across the city. Obviously I don't want to teleport Glory to my room—and there's still that "I aimed for a troll but ended up poofing away the money" issue, but if I could figure out how to focus the spell . . . Maybe it'll work if we double the witch factor and Tara helps to ground me.

The money smelled weird when I got it back, and it made all its friends in the cash register smell weird, too. —A

DIRECTIONS:
Keep yak cheese next to your skin. Approach the one that you would like to send elsewhere and cover them with Aradia's dust. Say:

DISCEDE!
TRANSLATION:
BE GONE!

TOOLS AND INGREDIENTS:
- ARADIA'S DUST
- YAK CHEESE

Aradia is said to have gone to Tibet in her many travels, where she worked with monks to refine a powder said to be imbued with the essence of time. Those monks must still be busy because it's not a difficult ingredient to find. Or maybe they just happen to have all the time in the world? Who knows.

I have no explanation for the cheese.
—Willow

February 13, 2001

The teleportation spell worked on Glory, so yay! Unfortunately, there have been some side effects, like nosebleeds, and ginormous headaches. Do the bands at the Bronze always play their instruments at approximately ten thousand decibels? Cause that's kind of what it felt like the other night.

As much as I hate to admit it, I guess I'm just not ready for that level of witchwork. Or at least I need to go into these spells with a better awareness of their potential consequences. Take that disastrous Willow will-enacting magick I tried to do last year—it seems like it's turned into the spell that won't stop giving.

Buffy says that Spike tried to tell her that he was in love with her. There was a stakeout, and a flask, and he went on about the Ramones, and now I'm worried that his fixation might be a lingering effect of the whole fake wedding fiasco. She asked me to revoke his all-access pass to the Summers house. To be honest, with all the use this spell gets, I think we should just call it the Buffy Special.

I remember the first time that I did it, back when Angelus needed de-inviting, and how I spent two hours going over all the ingredients and practicing the four lines of Latin. Now it's all old hat . . . I guess I have grown.

Maybe I shouldn't be so hard on myself about not being up to teleportation spells. Maybe one day, Future Willow will look back on all this and go, "Remember when teleportation spells gave me a headache? Now I think I'll teleport to [insert scenic venue here] and go for a brisk jog."

Or a brisk sit. That sounds more likely.

The whole seducing thing was way more suave-like than you're making it sound here —S

No. It wasn't. And I don't like the Ramones. —B

DE-INVITATION SPELL

TOOLS AND INGREDIENTS:

- moss
  (any kind of moss)

CRUCIFIXES

HOLY WATER

DIRECTIONS:

After hanging a crucifix in every entryway used by the undead spirit that you wish to revoke, sprinkle holy water across each threshold. While burning the moss, complete the following incantation:

> ILLA TENET NULLO REGNA INSIPIENTIUM.
>
> HIC EST INANIMATUM ET ENS NON AMBULANT.
>
> PURGA CAELI IANITRIX.
>
> HICCE VERBIS CONSENSUS RESCISSUS ES.

TRANSLATION:

> LET THE INVOCATION OF THE UNWISE DISAPPEAR.
>
> LET THE SOULLESS BEING WALK HERE NO LONGER.
>
> PURIFY THE AIR, GUARD THE DOOR.
>
> BY THESE UNANIMOUS WORDS, IT IS RESCINDED.

This is the first time I've ever seen the translation. Does anyone else feel like it's a little invitation shame-y? I'm not unwise . . .
—B

April 17, 2001

Buffy's mom died. I can't believe that I'm writing this. She came through the surgery fine, was up and Joyce-y again, and then Buffy came home and found her on the couch. Everything changed in an instant.

We're all in shock and dealing with what's happened in different ways; Xander's eaten five times his body weight in casserole, and I think I've gone home to visit my mother more often in the past few days than during my entire freshman year of college. I've even started keeping a separate, regular, non-magickal diary again, as a way of making sure every moment counts.

Dawn is having a hard time, which is, you know, to be expected. She said she didn't want to go back to a Joyce-less house right after the funeral service, so Tara and I let her spend the night at our place. It didn't take long to figure out what Dawn was after; she asked us to do a spell to bring her mother back. Tara was quick with the Wicca warnings about how we take an oath not to disrupt the natural order of things, because she's kind and good and gentle like that. I know she's probably right, but I still found myself biting my tongue. Because from where I'm sitting, the "natural order of things"—one where a girl who has already died once to keep the world safe still loses her mother at age twenty—is looking pretty damn unnatural.

So the next morning, before I left for class, I nudged Dawn toward reading DiPastori's <u>History of Witchcraft</u>. I didn't think that she'd be able to get very far with it—sure, there's a chapter on resurrection, but it's more a recap of other books on the subject, all of which are chock-full of difficult translations and obscure ingredients. I wanted to give her a distraction, something to give her a sense of control while she waited for time to stitch herself back together.

I don't know how, but she did a spell. Buffy says Dawn ripped up the summoning picture before they saw what was at the door, but something came back. This morning, Dawn showed up at our door holding Tara's copy of the DiPastori and looking apologetic. Tara just took it, gave her a hug, and then left for her English class. But before I followed, Dawn must have been able to tell that I had questions, because she handed me a piece of paper and said, "It felt weird just throwing it away."

I don't even want to know how Dawn got some of these ingredients (there are Ghora demons in Sunnydale?), but it is fascinating. And obviously very dark. Tara thinks that if we dive into stuff like this, we'll manipulate the world until it comes unglued . . . and maybe she's right. But there has to be a way for a witch to move beyond that, to figure out a way to glue everything back together—a witch who can make sure that the world treats her friends fairly.

A Resurrection Spell

Tools and Ingredients:
- Grave dirt (of the deceased)
- Chicken blood
- Egg of a Ghora demon
- Photo of the one you want to bring back
- Candles (5)
- Cauldron

Directions:

Cast a circle with chicken blood, and anchor it with your five lit candles. Place your cauldron in the center, and add the dirt from the deceased's grave and the contents of the Ghora egg.

Chant the following:

Osiris, giver of darkness,
Taker of life, god of gods, accept my offering.
Bone, flesh, breath.
Yours eternally.
Bone, flesh, breath.
I beg of you, return to me.

SPELLS TO CAUSE PAIN
(Adapted from <u>Darkest Magick</u>)

May 1, 2001

Glory hurt Tara. We had a fight about magick, Tara left for the carnival alone, and then Glory hurt her.

Buffy told me not to do anything crazy, and I'm not. It's simple—when someone hurts the one you love, and you have the power to hurt them back, you hurt them back. I'm tired of doing what Buffy says, tired of pretending that dark magick doesn't exist, tired of holding in my power.

Because I know the truth.

Life isn't fair. And sometimes the only way to fight that which is frightening is by being frightening yourself.

A Spell to Paralyze Your Victim

(Note: You'll need to have the victim in your sights for the final incantation, although the first incantation can be said at any point.)

Tools and Ingredients:
- ONYX
  (with a pentagram carved or etched into it)
- A PIECE OF AMBER
  (with insect trapped inside)

Directions:
Hold the onyx in the left hand, keeping it between your thumb and the space where the pointer and middle fingers meet; this connects the third eye and crown chakra points.

Hold the amber in the right hand in the same position. After lifting the stones to your eyes, recite the first incantation (below) to charge them with magickal power. Then, when you have eyes on your target, recite the second.

First Incantation:
Shiva, Euryale, Stheno, Cabrakan,
Footfalls hobbled, sails becalmed.
Cassiel, make worthy my eyes
The gorgon's gift to paralyze.

Second Incantation:
Kali, Hera, Kronos, Thonic,
Air like nectar, thick as onyx.
Cassiel, by your second star,
Hold mine victim as in tar.

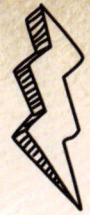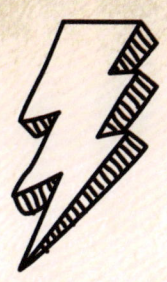

A SPELL TO STORE AND CONTROL LIGHTNING

TOOLS AND INGREDIENTS:

- ROD OF QUARTZ OR AMBER
- RAM'S WOOL (two lengths)
- COPPER MJÖLNIR PENDANT

DIRECTIONS:

Place one piece of wool on a flat surface and lie the rod across it. Holding the charm of Mjölnir in your left hand, use the second piece of wool to rub the rod while saying the following:

> Fill me with the warmth of Thor,
> And banish the wicked
> As Odinsson banished Jörmungandr
> On the eve of Ragnarök.

Each pass of the wool will store more power within the caster for later release.

> Honestly, this is a little much. Couldn't touch doorknobs on dry days for months after casting this, but I did save a fortune on batteries. —W

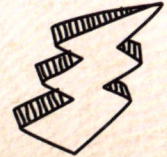

Invocation of Namazu
(A Spell to Shake the Earth)

This is a spell to cause massive vibrations in order to weaken the ground beneath your foe, but it can also be used to break things like glass. And hellgod bones.

Tools and Ingredients:
- Salt water
- Wooden rod (made from a tree that was killed by natural disaster)

POWDERED CATFISH BONES

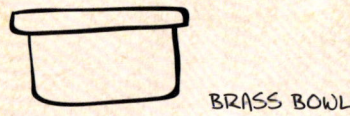
BRASS BOWL

Directions:
Pour an inch of salt water into your brass bowl. Add the powdered catfish bones, then hold the bowl in your left hand and recite the three-line incantation below.

> As Kashima sleeps
>
> Let Namazu stir
>
> And with fury thrash her tail.

Using the rod, strike the bowl and hum to match the resulting vibrations. When the sound has faded completely, drink the contents of the bowl.

You should now have the power to shake the earth.

Invocation of Serpents

(A spell that calls snakes to do your bidding)

Tools and Ingredients:

- Aloe (fresh)
- Musk Oil
- Black Pepper (ground)
- Saffron (dried)
- Vervain (dried)
- Velvet Pouch 
- Khul's Amulet

Directions:
Grind together the aloe, pepper, musk, vervain, and saffron—all herbs used in spells for summoning spirits. Place the resulting powder in a velvet pouch with Khul's amulet. Upon saying the following words, your target will be immobilized by snake spirits.

Spirit of serpents now appear

Hissing, writhing, striking near

MAY 8, 2001

Sometimes, in my nightmares, we are back in this RV, there are no rest stops for eight hundred miles, and Anya is cooking shrimp. —X

Attacking Glory did nothing. All that dark magick, and I barely even dinged her makeup. Tara is still weak and helpless and so not Tara it makes me want to cry.

It's my fault. It's *all* my fault. If I hadn't flown off the handle at Tara when she said I was frightening, I would have been with her. I could have protected her. I wouldn't have gone after Glory, and Glory wouldn't have come after us and found out that Dawn is the Key.

Buffy is panicking. None of us know what to do, which is why we're all sitting in a Winnebago that smelled like canned meat product before Anya pulled out the Spam and heading toward who knows where. I don't even want to know how Spike got his hands on this lovely piece of American history.

I'm trying to find a barrier spell to give us a little extra defense, but I don't know how to make it mobile . . . if you can even call thirty miles an hour mobile. There are several options, many that use light magick, but I can still feel the remnants of the dark magick tugging at the edges of my brain, telling me that the power I used to do the paralysis spell on Glory could work for us here, and be stronger than anything else I could come up with on the fly.

I still have the onyx and amber. It would be easy.

But . . . I'll keep looking.

I don't know, I think it was of fun! . . . Apart from the being chased by Glory part and the rain of arrows part hey! Never need to go to Medieval Times now. —D

Won it at poker from a chaos demon. They actually smell a lot like canned meat product, so . . . makes sense. —S

SHOOT ME NOW

A Barrier Spell
(A spell to create an impenetrable wall between you and a force that wishes you harm)

Tools and Ingredients:
- Any stone that can grant powers of the earth (a piece of onyx, carved with a pentagram, will work again in a pinch)
- Any stone with powers of fire (amber, with insect trapped inside)

Directions:
Hold stones tight, one in each hand. Visualize the power arcing up from your body and providing a protective dome around whatever you wish to protect.

> Enemies high and tall.
>
> Circling arms, raise a wall.

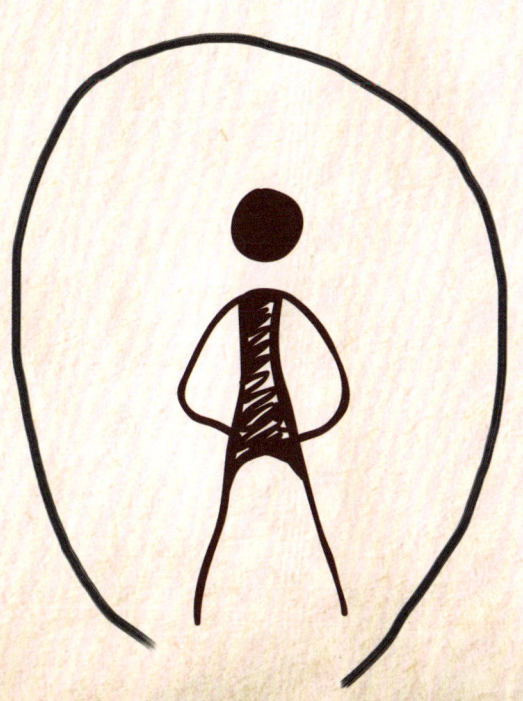

May 15, 2001

I had to use the dark spell. Before I could find something else, we were interrupted by a group of horse-riding religious types who shot at us with arrows and cornered us in an abandoned gas station in the middle of nowhere. Giles is hurt, Glory found Dawn, and Buffy has gone catatonic. In retrospect, our time in the RV is looking like a relaxing adventure full of happy, joyride-y fun.

 We've tried everything to snap Buffy out of it. Yelling, finger snapping—and, if you're Spike, hitting—but nothing's worked. Until, all at once, I felt a sense of . . . purpose and surety come over me. Maybe it was the gas fumes, but I knew that we all needed to get back to Sunnydale, and that I needed to be the one to take charge of getting Buffy back so that we could fix Tara and save Dawn . . . and maybe, while we were at it, try to figure out what the connection is between Glory and Ben. Spike seems to think that they are connected in some way, but his idea of a therapeutic technique is to punch a girl having a mental breakdown in the face, so maybe we'll just take that with a grain of salt.

 There are a lot of mindwalking spells out there, but again—something's telling me to go back to Cloutier. While most of his work was devoted to spells that turned astral projection outward, I feel like there might be a way to adapt his ingredients and methods to turn the focus inward, into someone else's subconscious. Instead of the Oil of Abramelin—I shouldn't need demon protection—I'll use a poppy to help access the dream world, and turn the whole thing into a kind of talisman that can journey with me.

 It's worth a shot. You know what they say—if you don't try, you're definitely going to be destroyed by a hellgod.

See? She gets it. —D

If we survive the First, remind me to take you on a real vacation. —B

Ben was Glory's brother, right? —X

*Bloody hell, Harris. I **will** bite you. —S*

MINDWALKING
(OR, A SPELL TO HOP IN YOUR BEST FRIEND'S MIND AND SNAP HER OUT OF AN ILL-TIMED CATATONIA)

TOOLS AND INGREDIENTS:
- ACACIA (dried)
- CARDAMOM (dried)
- LEATHER POUCH

WHITE CANDLES (3)

VIOLET (dried)

POPPY SEEDPOD

DIRECTIONS:

Grind the acacia, cardamom, and violet, and then add the powder mixture to a leather pouch that contains one poppy seed pod. Find a way to keep the pouch on your person (a necklace is often the most secure).

With three lit candles to help guide you, sit across from the person whose mind you wish to enter. Look into their eyes and visualize a curtain behind their eyes. You will know when they are ready to let you step behind it.

May 22, 2001

The mindwalking spell worked. After déjà vu-ing around in the Buffy brain for a few hours and pulling her out from a dip in its three-star pity pool of "I killed my sister," I was able to convince her that the only way she would be responsible for killing Dawn is if she didn't snap out of it and help us fight Glory.

Everything is still terrible. Tara's been acting extra agitated lately—I could barely stand to see her like this before without wanting to crumple up into a guilty little ball, and it's worse now that I can barely keep her calm, even with the medication. There has to be a way to fix this; I don't care what rules I have to bend.

Giles says that if Glory manages to start the ritual to open all the hell dimensions, the only way to stop it is to kill Dawn. At least getting Buffy back still feels like a victory. Sure, a speck of victory—more like victory lint—but it's something. And I'm going to use the momentum from that victory to create more specks of victory until it's just one big ball of victory barreling into Glory like a ton of lint.

I mean bricks. Ton of bricks. Bricks would be more helpful.

I did this! I hit her with a ton of bricks! Man, I feel cool.—>

We've all been tasked with trying to come up with ways to impede Glory, and I think I might have a spell that could take back the minds that she's stolen, including Tara's. It might also make all our heads explode, but I suppose if that's appropriately timed, it would make for a good distraction. Oh, and did I mention that I might be a little telepathic now? Ever since doing the mindwalking spell, I can sense the others' thoughts, like shadows behind a screen. All it would take is a little nudge, and the screen would disappear, which is . . . exciterrifying. That is now a word.

I haven't said anything, because I'm not sure if it's a permanent thing or just a side effect . . . but I will keep an eye on it; the last time there was a bout of telepathy in the gang, it didn't go so well. Buffy says that I'm her big gun, which, hello, pressure, but I didn't fight her on it. I also didn't say anything when she was arguing with Giles about protecting Dawn till the end, even if Glory was successful in starting the ritual, though it was hard not to see where Giles was coming from.

I love Dawn. I don't want to lose Dawn, and I'm going to put my life on the line and do everything I can to make sure we don't. But if it comes down to it . . . and if it's the whole world or Dawn, I just don't see how Buffy is going to have any other choice.

That's why there was option C. Leap off a scaffold into a giant blobby pool of blue energy and be zapped back to life five months later. All part of the long game.—B

Still, I have to believe that Buffy will figure it out—she always does.
It's why she's the Chosen One.

A Spell to Reverse Mind Energy
(Getting Tara's Memories Back from Glory)

Tools and Ingredients:
- GOTU KOLA (dried and ground)
- SYLVITE CRYSTAL (small)
- CARNALLITE CRYSTAL (small)
- FISH LIVER OIL
- CANDLE
- BOWL

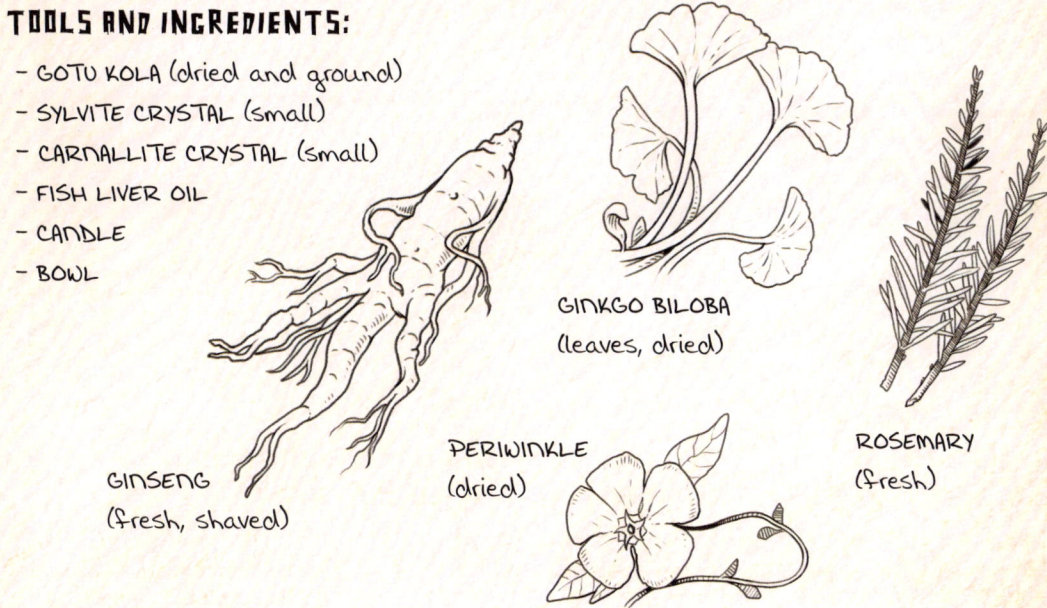

GINSENG (fresh, shaved)

GINKGO BILOBA (leaves, dried)

PERIWINKLE (dried)

ROSEMARY (fresh)

Directions:
Crush the herbal ingredients and the mineral ingredients into two separate batches of powder. Heat the oil in a bowl over the flame of the candle. When it begins to smoke, recite the following words to call upon the powers of healing deities:

> Snotra, Sága, Gefjon, Vör,
>
> From addled mind the thoughts restore.
>
> Asclepius, mend a mind broken
>
> From shards of what has been stolen.

Simultaneously pour both powders into the oil and stand back (it kind of makes a fireball).

Coat your hands with the resulting paste. Once coated, a caster should be able to transfer mental energy, memories, and even intellect between two subjects. This can effectively "cure" a person suffering from any sort of mental disorder, albeit at the cost of the mental state of the other person (which is Glory, so hello! Don't care).

BRINGING BUFFY BACK

OCTOBER 2, 2001

It's been almost five months since Buffy sacrificed herself to save the world. For five months, we've wondered if the person who should be here, smiling and laughing and punning in a non-Buffybot way that actually makes sense, is instead suffering in an unimaginable hell dimension. For five months, we've been stumbling around, trying to figure out how to protect Sunnydale without a Slayer while raising a happy (or at least healthy) Dawn without a mother or a sister. For five months, we've been trying to figure out how to fill the hole in every photo and conversation.

The truth is, after slogging through these past five months, we've realized that it's going to be impossible to do any of these things. And that's why, tonight, I'm going to bring Buffy back.

It's taken a while to round up the ingredients, but Anya was able to find the last ingredient, an urn of Osiris, on the internet. It took longer to get everyone on the same page; Xander is naturally a little jumpy, and I didn't want to argue with Tara so soon after I—somehow, miraculously—got her back, whole and as beautifully intelligent as ever, from Glory. But slowly, as time went by and the not-rightness of life without Buffy refused to diminish, we all agreed: It wasn't fair or natural the way Buffy died.

Everyone's looking to me. Xander made the "Boss of Us" plaque as a kind of joke, but I've used it for a little pick-me-up a lot these past few days, especially when it's been tempting to tell Giles to put a hold on going back to England until we see if the spell works. But I don't know how he'd react, or what he would say or do if something went wrong. And then there's Spike, our undead, sort-of-evil babysitter—every so often, he looks so haunted that I want to tell him to buck up, that there's a chance she could come back.

Still, I don't think it's going to go wrong. While I've never exactly been one with the self-confidence, I know that I can do this. I've been conserving my energy and keeping my nose to the books. I've kept some details close to my chest; Egyptian magick is known for the rigorous spiritual tests it demands of the casters, and the ingredients make me a little queasy, being all blood and dead things. I'm not sure what to expect when I go into the woods today for the vino de madre.

Whatever it is, though, it's worth it.

The world owes us our friend. The world owes Buffy a happy ending.

I don't know. I kind of liked her marzipan joke. —D

And the Backstreet Boys lunchbox! . . . And now that I'm not bound by a fiancé-fiancée secrecy contract, it wasn't for a friend. It was for Xander. —A

I prefer "vampire bodyguard." And there are still days where I'm still of a mind to kill you all for not telling me, so thanks. —G

A Spell to Call an Innocent Creature for Sacrifice

(Or, Something I Can't Think About Too Much)

Tools and Ingredients:
- Daisy seeds
- Dandelion seeds
- White Carnation seeds (or baby's breath seeds)
- Daffodil seeds

Directions:
After bathing, dress in garb of pure white. Go to a place of natural beauty. In the full light of day, after scattering the seeds across the earth, call upon the spirits of innocence with the following words:

> Adonai, Helomi, Pine.
>
> Adonai, Helomi, Pine.
>
> The gods do command thee from thy majesty.
>
> O Mappa Laman, Adonai, Helomi,
>
> Come forward, blessed one,
>
> Know your calling.
>
> Come forward, blessed one.

Please tell me that this is here because you watched Bambi later that night. —D

A being of clean heart should approach. Using a knife that you've blessed with a blue flame, take your sacrifice. After gathering the heart's blood, the vino de madre, thank the animal for its offering so that the gift remains consecrated with the following words:

> Adonai, Helomi, Pine,
>
> Divine creature, child of Elomina,
>
> Accept our humble gratitude for your offering
>
> In death, you give life.
>
> May you find wings to the kingdom.

Flowers will forever mark the place of death.

THE INVOCATION OF OSIRIS
(TO RESURRECT A WARRIOR KILLED BY SUPERNATURAL FORCES)

TOOLS AND INGREDIENTS:

URN OF OSIRIS

BLACK CANDLES (3)

VINO DE MADRE MARKINGS
(the blood of an innocent creature)

DIRECTIONS:

When Mercury is in retrograde, gather four who knew the warrior during his or her lifetime and go to the fallen's grave at midnight. The one who will be directly beseeching Osiris should hold his urn, while the others each hold one lit black candle to guide the caster's work.

The beseecher should begin to recite the invocation, pouring the vino de madre into Osiris's urn. Once the urn is full, use the blood to mark his or her face as shown and say:

> **Osiris, keeper of the gate, master of all fate, hear us.**
>
> **Before time and after.**
>
> **Before knowing and nothing.**
>
> **Accept our offering. Know our prayer.**

Pour the remaining blood at the head of the warrior's grave.

> **Osiris, here lies the warrior of the people. Let her cross over!**

The spirits of the underworld will begin to weigh your soul to determine if your request is worthy of Osiris's blessing.

OCTOBER 9, 2001

I did it. It feels like my hands have been shaking ever since, but I did it. I asked Osiris to bring my friend back, and he said "Okay, Willow. You seem like a good, powerful witch-egg. Here you go."

It's taking Buffy a while to adjust. That's natural. And when someone does a spell of that magnitude, it's expected that there are going to be consequences, magickal and otherwise. Sure, we happened to thaumogenesis up a vengeful poltergeist, but we took care of that. It was nothing. It was child's play . . . although now that I'm thinking of what the poltergeist said about us being children, no, it wasn't child's play. It was responsible, newly bodacious witch's play.

We beat the Sunnydale system. I beat the Sunnydale system. And now I feel like I could do anything—when Tara and I were doing the spell to corporealize the screamy weird spirit, it's like in the middle of it, my power just took over and did it for me. It was instinctual. For the first time, it felt like I didn't even need her power. I don't know if we even needed the angelica. For a second, it felt like I was the magick, and it was one of the most profound experiences of my life.

After it was over, I wanted to tell Tara, but something about the way she wouldn't meet my eyes for a while as she quickly cleared up all evidence of our spell made me hold my tongue. She's been practicing since childhood, and yet she's never talked about anything like this happening to her. I wonder if this is how being the Slayer feels for Buffy. Or, how it will feel after she gets the hang of this whole "I'm alive again!" thing.

I wish that everyone would stop looking for problems. Buffy even came into the Magic Box yesterday and thanked us for not abandoning her to a hell dimension. I mean, it lacked a little pep, but she's still shaking off the zombie willies, so it's fine.

I'm sure it's fine.

Why does it feel like there's still something missing?

A Spell to Make a Disembodied Spirit Corporeal

(Or, how to turn the ghost we made into something that Buffy can fight)

TOOLS AND INGREDIENTS:
- CANDLES
- ANGELICA

A classic in the exorcism department, angelica is good for the spirits who want to cause trouble. So most spirits we know. Still watching for a friendly ghost.

DIRECTIONS:

In a room lit only by candles, two casters involved in the original spell should join hands and say the following in tandem:

Child of words, hear thy makers.
Child of words, we entreat.
With our actions we did make thee,
To our voices wilt though bend.

With our potions, thou took motive,
With our motions, came to pass.
We rescind no past devotions,
Give thee substance, give thee mass.

MAGIC POV

I came up with this incantation myself! Thinking of submitting it to the UC Sunnydale literary magazine. Which is just called <u>Words</u>.

—Willow

A MAGICKAL HISTORY OF THE EVIL TRIO
Written by Andrew Wells

Gentle readers. I have been given a quest by the resident Wicca of this house where I have been kindly imprisoned for my own protection. While they are embroiled in their grueling fight to banish the First Evil and save us from the Death that will merely begin by the eating of our bottoms, I have been given a side quest. The important kind. The kind that, if you don't complete, you will never get the special cut scene that lets you truly understand the game you've just played.

> I mostly told Andrew to do this so he'd stop bugging everyone to let him read the book, but even so, this is ... south of helpful. But he looked so hopeful that I am making a big show of putting it in the book. I am writing on a Post-it. Tra la la. Okay, he's gone.
> —Willow

Buffy thinks it is better that I not gaze upon the spell book that they have all been passing around; as a man who once gave into the siren's call of crime, there is concern it will burn out my eyeballs. Instead, Willow has requested that I use my flirtation with the dark side to add to their knowledge by sharing the secrets that I was once privy to as a member of that evil Sunnydale group of legend: the Trio.

It was sunny the day the Trio decided to swear to their sacred covenant ... or it may have been cloudy, I don't know, for we were in a basement. Warren the Worst had just finished defeating Jonathan and me at Monopoly, that classic game that confounds men and tests their worth, when he said the words that would chisel our names in the great annals of Buffy's archnemeses.

"Hey, you wanna team up and take over Sunnydale?" he said, his voice rumbling in time with the sound of a pair of jeans that his mother had put into the dryer with the belt still attached. "I accept your call to arms," I said bravely, while my comrade and unjust owner of Park Place, Jonathan, just said, "Okay."

With great determination, we forged a list of principles that would guide our path forward:

THOV SHALT CONTROL THE WEATHER.
THOV SHALT MINIATVRIZE FORT KNOX.
THOV SHALT CONJVRE FAKE I.D.S.
GIRLS.
GIRLS.
THOV SHALT ... DO SOMETHING WITH GORILLAS.

(THIS WAS WARREN'S THING. I DON'T REALLY VNDERSTAND.)

Our most important task, however, was so important that it could not be named (except when needed so that we all knew what our goals and aspirations for the day were). That task was: Thou shalt conquer Sunnydale by defeating the Slayer.

With that in mind, we devised a cunning set of tests for our greatest enemy, ones that would compel us to delve deep into the murky realm of magick. While I have sworn a sacred oath to impart that knowledge here, be forewarned: This magick is what made me the cursed, bloodstained man I am today—a man who must live his life half in shadow, half in the light, and half in a sleeping bag at the end of the hallway, where he is trod upon by acolytes of the woman he once attacked, and where no one appreciates his movie night suggestions.

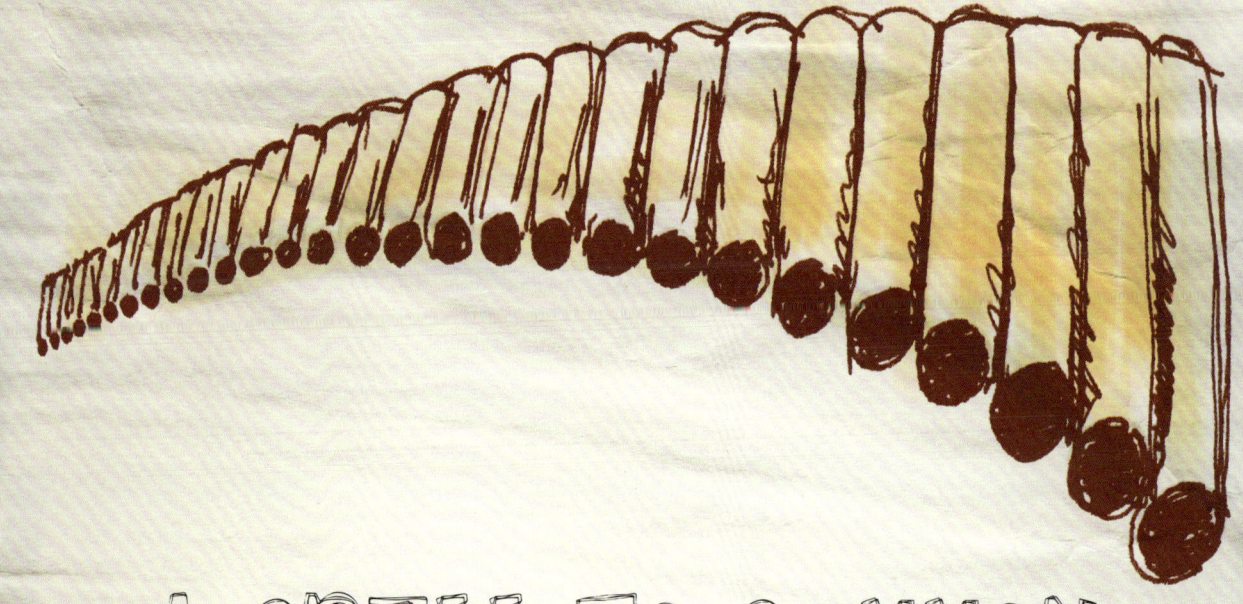

A Spell to Summon a Demon via Wind Instrument

(This spell summons a demon. With a wind instrument.)

Tools and Ingredients:
- Pan flute

Directions:
Bring the pan flute to your lips and play the mournful tones that summon demonkind. It could be any tune, really. I started out trying to play the theme from <u>Jaws</u>, but then just sort of went with what I felt.

You used a magickal artifact to call a demon, Andrew. This isn't a spell.
—W

Okay, but it's my story, so I need to be included. Otherwise, it would be like <u>Star Wars</u> without Han Solo. <u>Indiana Jones</u> without Indiana. James Bond movies without Bond, who is of course always played by the one and only Timothy Dalton.
—Andrew

THE CURSE OF ZURVAN, I THINK
(A SPELL TO CREATE AN IMPOSSIBLE TASK)

This spell uses the all the awesome powers of the universe to make one tiny thing really, really hard. Pretty sure someone cast this on me at birth. Probably Tucker, my lame-o older brother.

TOOLS AND INGREDIENTS:

- Golden Bowl of Zurvan (I think)
- Paper with the eternity symbol drawn on it, for offering
- A plant with thorns
- An object that the cursed once touched
- Red chalky stuff?

Jonathan's magic bone

Milk thistle (he said it was for perseverance)

DIRECTIONS:

The wizard shall draw a triangle on the ground—or on the carpet of a van—with the red chalky stuff. In the center, the wizard shall place a Golden Bowl of Zurvan (I think) and add the milk thistle and thorny plant.

Then, the wizard shall put flame to the paper and make an offering to Zurvan (I think), and say the following.

Latin, Latin, Latin, Latin.

Latin, Latin, Magic Bone, Latin.

(Sorry, I don't really remember what he said—I wish there were more spells in Klingon. Those I could have remembered.)
—Andrew

Once the incantation is complete, the time loop will take effect as soon as the cursed one fails to complete a task.

A Spell to Take on the Appearance of a Demon

Jonathan turned himself into a big muscly guy with this one. But keep in mind that you will not have any of the supercool demon powers, so really, my spell was better and I should have been declared the winner of the tournament.

Tools and Ingredients:

- Powdered Horn Of The Demon whose form you'd like to take (In this case, Reddus wrestlerus demonus)
- Demon stone
- Soda, at room temperature (Or probably any other liquid. This is just what was in the van.)
- Chalice

Directions:

Place your demon stone at the bottom of a chalice, and cover with liquid. Sprinkle in the powdered demon horn and repeat the following words:

Azeban, Anansi, Amaguq, Jafar, ← I don't know this deity. Wait, is he from that movie where everyone's punished for not taking enough treasure from that cave? —A

Grant me your form so that I may deceive mine enemies.

Oh, and when you want it to end, just say:

Let the spell be ended.

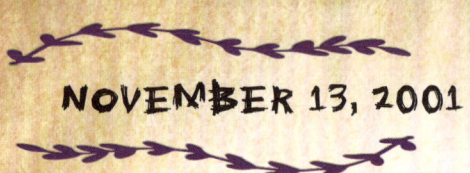
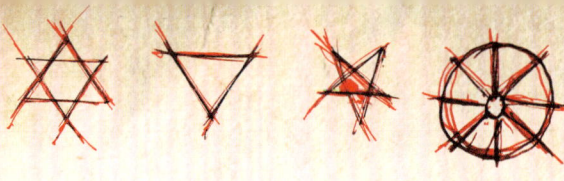

NOVEMBER 13, 2001

Yesterday, Tara told me that I was using too much magic. At first, I didn't understand what she was saying, or why she was looking at me like I had just said we should see if Ben and Glory wanted to pop over for tea. But then it sunk in—she was telling me that she knew I had used a forgetting spell on her. She said if I couldn't go a week without magic, then she would leave me. I don't think I could take that, not ever, but especially not right now, when I'm still trying to find the words to apologize to Buffy for ripping her out of heaven.

I want to fix things, both with her and with Buffy. But how will my going cold turkey help any of us? How would I help us fight whatever new supernatural thing is currently messing with Buffy? Sure, back in high school I could hack into databases and flip through microfilm, but when it came to actually being useful in a life-and-death kind of way? Not so much. Old Willow just sat in the library waiting for people to come back and tell her how the real hero stuff went.

But now, no matter what Giles says about me being a "rank, arrogant amateur," I know that there aren't many people on Earth who can do what I can do. I'm strong, and I'm powerful, and I'm the only thing that got the group through those five months when Buffy was gone. I fixed the Buffybot time and time again, and yes, maybe I miscalculated whether Buffy needed saving, but my intentions were good and I got the job done. I raised the actual dead. I kept us from falling apart, and by using this bigger forgetting spell to press the reset button, I'll keep us from falling apart again.

After this, I'll do what Tara asked and abstain for a week. I will get dressed the old-fashioned way, even if it means going back to searching through piles of unfolded laundry for the least-wrinkled pair of jeans. I'll look up information using a table of contents. I will ignore the power that thrums through my veins.

And then we can all start over. I will reintroduce the magick I use in front of Tara gradually, so as not to unnerve her again, and Buffy will forget heaven and can stop having to force a smile every time she catches one of us looking. (I should have known. How could I not have known?)

A blank slate. That's all I want. And then, this time, I'll get it right.

> TO GUARD AGAINST MEMORY SPELLS:
> 1. MAKE SURE YOUR I.D. IS UP TO DATE AND ON YOUR PERSON AT ALL TIMES.
> 2. IF YOU CAN'T BELIEVE SOMEONE WOULD NAME THEIR SON "RANDY GILES," THEY PROBABLY DIDN'T.
> 3. FOR THE LOVE OF ALL THAT IS HOLY, ANYA, DON'T KISS ANYONE!   —XANDER

TABULA RASA
(A SPELL FOR FORGETTING)

QUARTZ CRYSTAL

TOOLS AND INGREDIENTS:
- ONE QUARTZ CRYSTAL (free of imperfection)
- LETHE'S BRAMBLE (one sprig*)

*my books say the size is important, as forgetting spells can be very temperamental. It was obviously too small when I used it before, so maybe just a larger sprig this time?

LETHE'S BRAMBLE
Named after the Hadean river that caused forgetfulness in all who drank its water, this magickal flower is used to enhance spells of memory loss and mind control. According to Dawnie, it also "kind of makes nice potpourri."

DIRECTIONS:
Place sprig of Lethe's bramble in a location where it will be able to burn for several hours (a fireplace is ideal). Light one end of the herb until it nurtures a small, smoldering flame, and then use it to darken one end of the crystal, all while saying:

> LET LETHE'S BRAMBLE DO ITS CHORE.
>
> PURGE THEIR MINDS OF MEMORIES GRIM,
>
> OF PAINS FROM RECENT SLIGHTS AND SINS.
>
> WHEN THE FIRE BURNS OUT, WHEN THE CRYSTAL TURNS BLACK,
>
> THE SPELL WILL BE CAST.
>
> TABULA RASA, TABULA RASA, TABULA RASA.

Keep the crystal on your person. As long as those you intend to make forget are in your vicinity when Lethe's bramble turns to ash, the forgetting spell will be complete.

A SPELL FOR SUMMONING YOUR OWN PIT OF HELL

Eats engagement rings

MAGIC

Anya made me include this, "or else who might know what kind of fresh, hippity-hoppity cotton-tailed hell could be unleashed the next time." For the record, this newly dumped witch thinks a roomful of bunnies sounds kind of nice right now. —Willow

Bara bara himble gemination
These words call the furry little freaks.

Hible abri, abri voyon
This just makes the fluffers multiply, and threaten the cash register.

Avatas vega mata marai
Makes the Easter-themed hellscape disappear, once and for all.

November 20, 2001

Tara moved out. The Tabula Rasa spell backfired, and when we all regained the memories of who we were, there was no denying what I had tried to do. She's been ignoring my calls, so I've had no way to explain that I was just trying to fix us. That someone had to fix us.

I don't know how to sleep when she's not here. I've never lived in this house without her; on the nights when Buffy is out and Dawn is at a friend's, I don't know what to do with myself.

But I've been trying to look on the . . . I'm not going to call it the bright side, but maybe just the side that isn't a big gaping void. Without Tara, there's no reason to hide the amount of magick I'm doing. The Scooby Gang has been doing a lot of research lately, trying to figure out who has been robbing banks and museums and fiddling with Buffy's life, and I thought, hey, wouldn't it be so much easier if I could just zap all this information into my brain and flip through it there? Kind of like witch hacking. I think there might even be a way to zap the text directly from your brain to paper in a spooky, kooky Kinko's kind of deal.

Until last night, I'd never been able to get the word-absorbing effects of the spell to last longer than five minutes. But then I realized that the key was to bring in something I could wear, something that I could charge with power. A ring with embedded stones could even be self-sustaining. And then, with enough practice, you might be able to do it without wearing the ring at all.

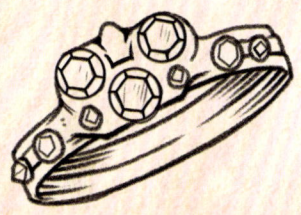

DE-RATTING SPELL
ATTEMPT NUMBER FOUR
(SUCCESS!)

NOVEMBER 27, 2001

I can't believe it. After three years and a magic shop's worth of herbs, I finally figured out how to fix Amy. Ironically, it didn't even require an elaborate spell. When I was practicing my new word-absorbing powers on the coven forums, I came across a link to an article about an Italian sorcerer who discovered that the plague of rats infesting his city was actually a vengeful coven of witches. He stopped them by forcing them to return to their human form. I called his research to me by saying "Rivili!"—thank you, Internet community of Italian covens—and two seconds later, presto! A naked, non-rat Amy on my bed.

It's been nice to have a magickally inclined friend around again, one who doesn't look at me as if I've sprouted three heads every time I have a little fun with dimensions and temporal folds. She convinced me to go to the Bronze last night, and we were able to completely change the vibe by zapping in elements from other Bronzes in other universes. Kind of wish I knew which Bronze the sheep came from. Maybe the one in a universe where the Bronze has Farm Night? Oh, or maybe it's a Sheep-Only Bronze, and they have little sheep drinks and play sheep pool and occasionally get taken into the alley by little sheep vampires before getting saved by the sheep Slayer.

Amy was doing some cool stuff, too... although definitely of the darker variety. When she made those two blowhard guys dance in cages, I recognized the spell from the book I used when I went up against Glory. They would have danced until they died—but, I mean, I know she wouldn't have let it go that far. And while I felt like I needed to join in with some black mojo to keep up with the witch party, I was in total control.

Tara was in the kitchen when we got home. My heart fluttered, and my first impulse was to kiss her hello. But then Amy started talking about what we had done, and I saw Tara's face harden with judgement. I felt ashamed, and then I felt angry for being ashamed—she left me. And besides, magick is nothing to be ashamed of. It's beautiful and powerful and makes me useful.

That look on her face was why I went out with Amy again, even after I said I wouldn't have another night like that for a while. I'm glad I did—Amy took me to meet a warlock named Rack. At first I was a little put off by his whole vibe, which for lack of a better word was... cockroach-y. But once he started sharing his magick, that all faded away. I'm not sure how long I was there, or how I got home. All I know is that for a brief, glittering patch of time, I didn't feel empty because Tara had left me, or scared that she would never speak to me again, or nervous that what everyone was accusing me of might be true. All I felt was euphoria, a connectedness to magick in its purest, most elemental form.

The only hard part is coming back down. Coming back to the real world.

Puffy, the Sheep Vampire Slayer. It strikes fear in my heart. —X

So not a fan of this girl. She better steer clear from here on out. —B

NOVEMBER 28, 2001

My hand is shaking so much that I can hardly write. I almost got Dawnie killed last night. We were going to a movie, and Dawn started telling me about hanging out with Tara, and suddenly I couldn't take it anymore; I needed to disappear into Rack's magick, to be in that blank floaty space that is free of ex-girlfriends and their new apartments and boxes of clothes that still smell like them.

I thought it would just be a moment—a quick press of the Cool Willow reset button. But it all went wrong. Somehow, I summoned a demon, and in the process of running away, I crashed our car and Dawn broke her arm.

It could have been worse. Buffy knows that it could have been worse, too, but she's gone into full let's-forgive-and-fix-this mode, which is surprising. I mean, I'm grateful, but I don't feel like I deserve it. This morning she went on a mini-rampage, cleaning out all of my magick supplies—the effigies, the cards, the crystals, the candles—everything.

I almost told her to take this book, too. After all, everyone was right. I wasn't able to control it. I couldn't stop. I hurt people that I care about—not just Dawn, but also Tara, and everyone who lost their memory after I used Lethe's bramble. And everyone at the Bronze that night Amy and I let loose. It's a problem. It's . . . an addiction.

But when I opened my mouth to tell Buffy to look behind the philosophy books, something told me to stay silent. I also didn't say anything when she missed a box of general supplies on the bookshelf. What if something happens and I need it? What if we're in trouble and everyone needs Super Willow? Not Sad, Lonely, Weak Willow.

So, I held my tongue. But I swear—I'm not going to do any more spells.

> HEY. HEY YOU, MAGICK GIRL. READ THIS IF YOU'RE EVER TEMPTED TO GET CRAZY WITH THE DARK MAGICK AGAIN. I MEAN IT. SEE MY SERIOUS FACE. I KNOW YOU CAN'T REALLY BECAUSE THIS IS A POST-IT BUT IT LOOKS LIKE THIS:
>
> —Willow

A SPELL TO NOT DO SPELLS ANYMORE
(NOT EVEN IF SOMEONE ASKS YOU TO)

TOOLS AND INGREDIENTS:

- SHAME
- DISGUST
- DESPAIR

DIRECTIONS:

Mix ingredients together in the crucible of your body. Chant aloud the names of the people you've hurt. Call Tara, hear it ring forever. Walk by Dawn's room and see how much she hates you now. Fail to understand why Buffy is being so nice.

Feel like the world is ending.

Repeat, ad infinitum.

November 29, 2001

Yesterday was my first day without magick, and so of course that was the day that the universe went, "Hey! How about you get kidnapped." It turns out the big, bad supernatural force that has been messing with Buffy is actually just three fairly nerdy guys with too much time on their hands and one shared inferiority complex. Robot-Boy Warren, Devil Dogs Jr. Andrew, and He-Should-Know-Better Jonathan have teamed up to wreak havoc and live out their revenge fantasies.

It was so tempting to do a spell that would paralyze them, or—better yet—make them invisible forever, but I didn't. I did things the old-fashioned way. The slow, painful, my-head's-killing-me-and-my-feet-will-fall-off way. I can't believe that this is how I used to do things all the time. That night, however, when I was about to fall asleep, I thought, "Tara would be proud of me." It's the first time I've thought that in a while.

December 8, 2001

I almost slipped up. Amy came by the house to pick up her cage as a weird memento, and before she left, she jolted me with magick. I could feel it tingling beneath my skin the entire rest of the day, eager to be used to speed up the process of figuring out what was going on at Doublemeat Palace. I almost caved; if ever there's a moment for a combustion spell, it's probably when a demon is spitting poison at you. After it was all over, though, and after Amy's magick had left my system, I felt a new kind of euphoria take hold. I was proud that I resisted... and angry that Amy tried to derail me. I've told her that she needs to stay away.

January 3, 2002

I ran into Tara today outside the Magic Box. She was holding a copy of the Brekenkrieg Grimoire, and for a second I was overcome with a powerful jealousy—here she tells me that I'm using too much magick, and she's just carrying around one of the most powerful texts on resurrection spells in history. But then I looked at her face, and suddenly I was babbling, telling her how I hadn't used magick in over a month—which I realized, somewhat startled, is the truth—and trying to subtly let her know how much I miss her without actually letting her know how much I miss her.

... I miss her.

January 19, 2002

The Buffy birthday curse struck again. Apparently Dawnie's been feeling lonely, and turned what was supposed to be a few hours of lighthearted birthday giggles into a forced sleepover brought to you by one of Anya's old partners in crime. Before we figured that out, Anya tried to bully me back into magick to help the gang figure out what was going on. Tara stood up for me. She told me that she was proud of me, and that I clearly didn't need the safety stash I had been keeping, because I held my ground when things got bad.

March 5, 2002

Xander left Anya at the altar yesterday. I . . . can't believe it. I've obviously had my differences with Anya, but I know that Xander loves her, and they seemed to be doing well.

We don't know where he is. We're all just sitting here, waiting for him to call, and wondering if we should break down Anya's door even though she says that she wants to be alone. I can't stop thinking of her standing on the stool while Tara and I buttoned up her wedding dress and asking Xander to protect her whole heart because it's all she has. I feel sick about how to help her, and then in between all the feeling sick, I'm feeling guilty. It's a sick-guilty-sick sandwich. Because while this is all a really sad time, a part of me has been dancing on air—but not literally!—ever since I saw Tara at the wedding. For the first time since she left, I feel like there might still be a chance for us.

April 30, 2002

Tara came back. There was coffee, and it was good coffee, and I thought, okay, maybe in a few months we can talk about what I can do to help her trust me again. And then suddenly, there she was standing in the doorway of my bedroom and asking me to kiss her and now she's lying beside me and I could cry. I think I am crying a little bit, because I don't deserve her. I don't deserve her forgiveness and her beauty and her grace. I don't deserve her whole heart, but she's giving it back to me anyway.

She says that she sent me a letter. She says that she went out to drop it in a mailbox and then, instead of turning around and going back to her apartment that was full of everything but Willow, she just kept walking. We don't know how it's going to work—she has a lease and we need to go slow when it comes to bringing magick back into our room and our relationship—but she's coming back. And I promise that I'll never do anything to make her want to leave again.

SPELLS TO END THE WORLD

I embraced my vengeance and the dark words of all those in pain for centuries traveled up my arms and all I do is think think think and it feels connected, a record of all that has come and all that will come, and I will kill him. I will kill all three of them. I will kill everyone.

　　　Blue shirt, blood from Tara's whole heart on my hands. Osiris saying no, no, no, not possible, not anymore, this is a natural death. If he were not dead, I would kill him, too. I would burn him alive from the inside out until there is nothing but a husk and Tara is in the doorway saying, "Can we just skip that part? Can you just be ki~

　　　Save Buffy. Need to save Buffy, use the bullet because there's a spell to find Tara's killer, I can feel it crawling behind my eyelids like a spider. There is nothing I do not know, not with the secrets of dark witches curled around my spine, making a nest in my marrow and the chambers of my heart. He was arrogant, they all were, and now they will all burn. Tara used to eat toast in the morning, but now she is there on the floor of our bedroom and what is the point? We will all be dust in the end, anyway. Time is inconsequential now.

　　　There is nothing I cannot do, no pain I cannot inflict. Buffy will try to stop me, but she will fail, and she will be happier after Proserpexa, happier back in the ground and in the peace I took her from.

　　　The world will be a cinder. It will burn until it is pure and we are all at rest.

I don't know how someone says sorry for this. I wanted to rip it all out—I did rip out a few pages—but then I knew that I had to leave it as a reminder of the kind of pain I can cause if I let myself lose control.

　　　　　　—Willow

ADIKIA'S OWN BLOOD

THIS MAGICK SHALL LEAD YOU TO THE KILLER YOU SEEK.

TOOLS AND INGREDIENTS:
Blood of the slain
Large paper or cloth
The item used to kill the slain (or a piece of it)

DIRECTIONS:

With the cloth before you, and bearing the instrument of death in one hand, scatter the blood of the slain across its surface. Raise your voice to Adikia, the goddess of injustice, and beseech her to guide you to he who has committed the grave offense:

Blood of the Slain, hear me.
Guide me to the killer.

SENTENCE OF THE LEMURE

It is said that there exists a powerful hex by the name of Lemure's Sentence, in which one with great power and righteousness—just or misguided—can torment one who has killed with the malignant souls of his victims. The subject is first asked if they have committed any sin and given the chance to confess. Upon denial, the witch should look into the accused's eyes and speak the word "reveal," which will summon any lemures who owe their existence to the subject's direct actions. It should be noted that the souls of the very recently deceased may not have had time to transition and will not torment the accused, and those who were killed but whose souls have found peace will likewise not answer the call.

A Spell to Haunt a Murderer
with the Souls of His Victims
—Willow

BROKK'S SILENCE

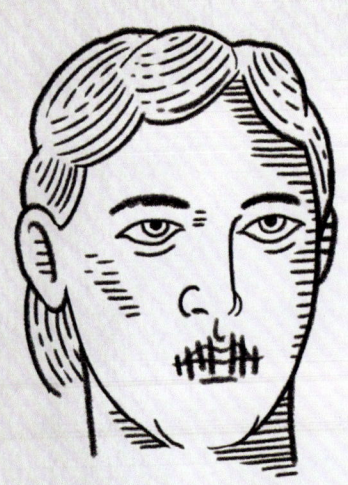

For those thou wish to curse with the quick cessation of speech, thou shalt take an item shaped like an awl and a piece of leather binding. Wrap the leather about the awl and say:

AS BROKK ONCE ENDED LOKI'S MOCKING,

EITRI BINDS YOU.

I AM TALKING.

FATE OF MARSYAS

(To Punish Those Who Hath Committed the Sin of Excessive Hubris)

TOOLS AND INGREDIENTS:

- WHITE PINE SHAVINGS
- FIVE REEDS
- A PIECE OF HUMAN SKIN
- BOWL
- FLUTE CRAFTED FROM WOOD

DIRECTIONS:

As you ponder the ravages of pride, fashion a pentagram from the five reeds and place a bowl in its center. Fill with the shavings of white pine and set them ablaze. Add the skin. As the flames grow, play a long, low note on the flute and then stop to intone:

MIGHTY APOLLO, HEAR ME.

THIS ONE IS AS CONCEITED MARSYAS.

LET THEIR FATES BE SHARED.

Break the flute and add to the blaze. Lean into the smoke. Inhale it. From that moment forth, you will have the power to strip the skin of those who exhibit excessive arrogance.

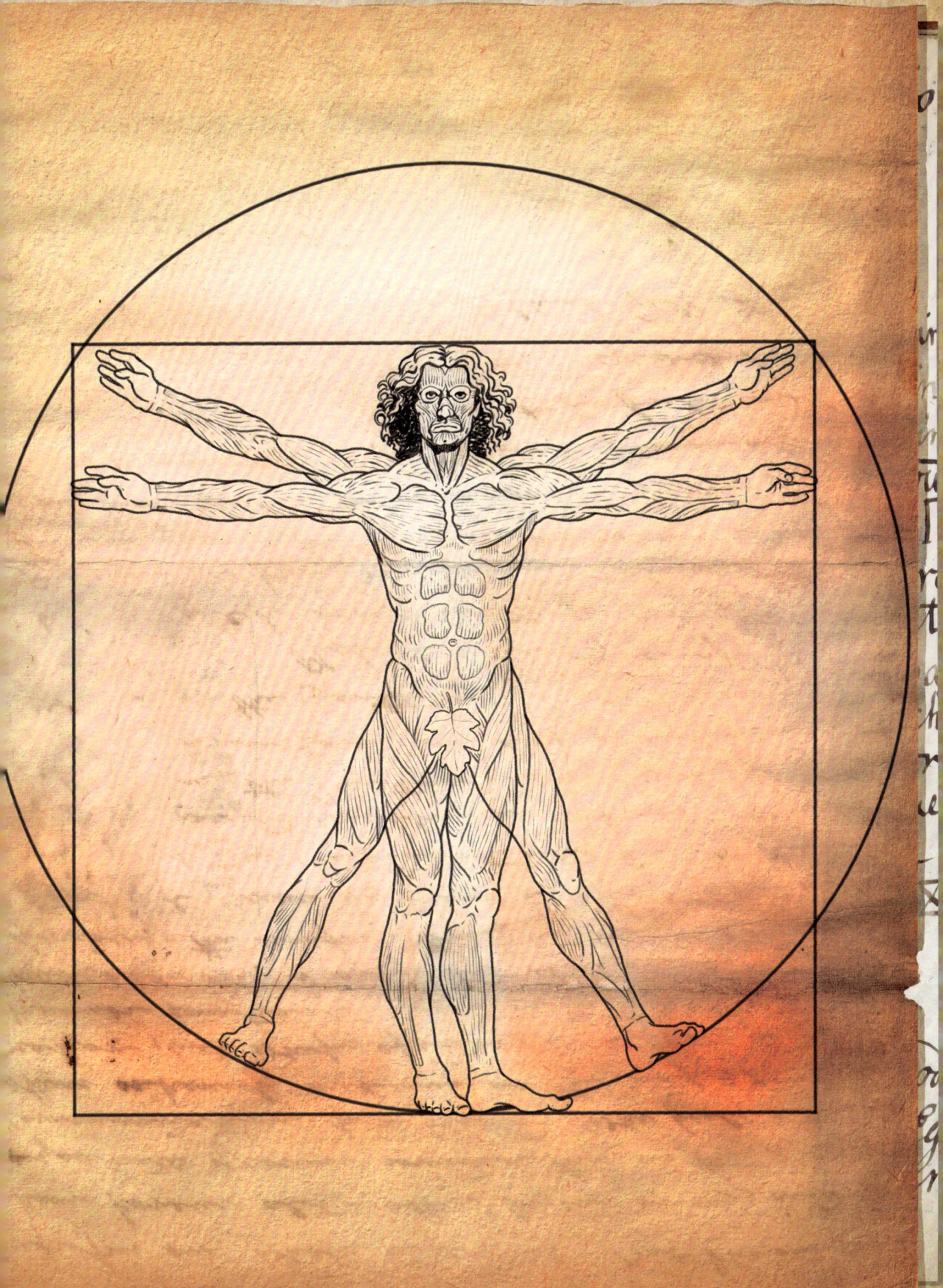

INVOCATION OF FIRE

Upon completion, you will be as of fire. From without, from within, from beginning to end, all is the same. Let it be so.

Tools and Ingredients:

- Large red cloth
- Beeswax candle
- Redwood bowl
- Piece of jasper
- Smoky quartz crystal
- Thistle
- Chili
- Ladybug
- Athame

DIRECTIONS:

Spread a large red cloth across the ground. From north to south, arrange the following items on its expanse: a candle made of beeswax, a bowl made of redwood, a piece of jasper, a piece of smoky quartz. Grind up the thistle, chili, and ladybug and place the powders into the bowl of redwood.

Light the candle and use it to set fire to the bowl's contents, all while saying the first verse of the incantation below. Say the second while heating an athame in the flames. Touch the quartz and jasper with the athame. Lay the blade down so that the point is facing south. After the fire burns out, cover your hands in the ashes and say the third verse.

This spell seemed like it might be useful, so I wrote it down again.
—Willow

FIRST VERSE:
Spirit of fire, come to us.

We will kindle the flames.

SECOND VERSE:
Spirit of fire, come to us.

We will make it burn.

THIRD VERSE:
We will kindle the fire.

Dance the magick circle round.

We will kindle the fire.

We will kindle the fire.

RAISE WARRIORS FROM THE EARTH

And the witch cast her enemies into a deep grave, full of the bones of ancestors past. As they clamored to escape, she whispered to the dead, bidding them to lend their withering flesh to her cause. Monsters sprung from the dirt around them, each one born from the tooth of a willing skeleton.

PROSERPEXA

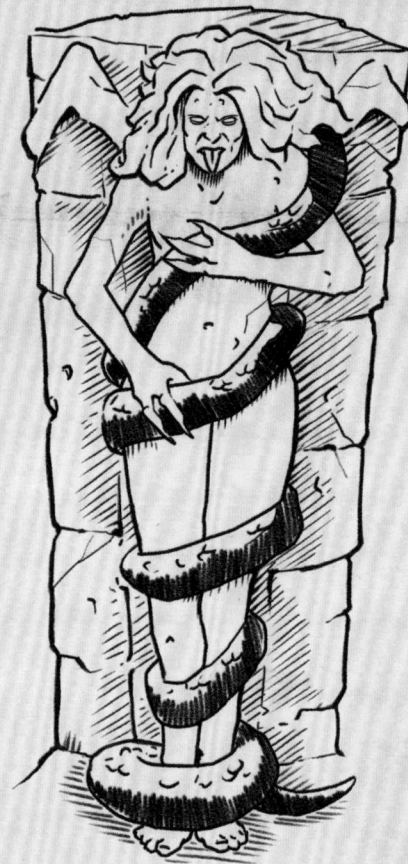

Finally, one of the more obscure Hellmouth cults was that of the worshippers of Proserpexa, who it is said wanted to drain the world of magickal energy and then use it to scorch planet Earth to a cinder. They attempted this in 1932, but were interrupted by an earthquake that historians believe had no relation to the rite they were hoping to perform.

Followers were to gather around Proserpexa's temple as a high priest spoke the incantation that would transfer their power to the she-demon's effigy. However, given that the effigy cannot store power, triggering Proserpexa required the full, coordinated participation of a powerful coven, something that the cult's ranks never managed to achieve.

September 24, 2002

When Giles first brought me to England, I thought it was to kill me, or to stash me in some deep mystical dungeon where my arms would be strapped to my chest and the world would be kept safe from Evil Willow. Instead, he brought me to a place that looks like a page out of an Austen novel and introduced me to a coven who have been tutoring me in natural magick. The scariest thing I've had to face is the fact that Giles is a person who goes horseback riding. A lot.

Still, as wonderful as the women in the coven are, they can't always hide their fear. Giles says that it isn't fear of me, it's more fear of the magick that I contain, the magick that has become my cross to bear for all the evil that I did . . . for all the evil that I became. As much as I would like to forget it, I can't. I couldn't even tear out all the pages of spells that I had catalogued in my despair. I need the reminder. I need that flayed man, that leering face of Proserpexa to keep me from ever going there again.

Tara wrote me a letter. Before she died, she told me that she had, but I had forgotten in the . . . in the everything. It showed up at Buffy's a few days after I was gone, and they forwarded it to Giles. He held onto it for a few weeks, but finally decided that I could handle reading it. He meant well, but I don't know that Tara's death will ever be something that I'll be able to "handle." I don't know how it will ever feel fair that I'm here and she's not. I haven't been able to read it yet. Maybe one day I will. For now, it's safely tucked into this journal.

Miss Hartness has been teaching me rituals through which I can become closer to Gaia, the ancestral mother of all life. I've been going through the motions of it for over a week without feeling any change, but then yesterday I managed to pull a flower up through the earth. Giles said that it came from Paraguay, and that its name was Flora kua alaya. It was pretty-instant tropics. I looked it up in the coven's encyclopedia later that night, and it said it was a symbol of healing.

I don't want to leave this place, where the only magickal demands are to ring up Gaia and pop flowers out of the ground. But there's something coming to the Hellmouth; I can feel it beneath the earth, waiting for its chance to sink its teeth into Buffy and Xander and Dawn and even Anya. I have to help them. I have to help my friends—I just hope that's what they still are.

Always.—B

Blessing of Gaia

Tools and Ingredients:

Nothing. I am the magick.

Directions:

Find an outdoor site that feels sacred to you. Sit and close your eyes. Breathing deeply, let your mind reach out to the verdant life that surrounds you. Realize that you are nature, that you are made up of the same elements and minerals that have created the Earth around you. Realize that it is all connected: the trees, the root systems, your breath, your body.

When the time feels right, say the following, silently or aloud:

> **Great Mother Gaia, I ask for your blessing.**
>
> **May you send me a helper, from far or near, to aid me in my journey of healing.**

Hey, isn't Gaia that lady who made all the cookies for the bake sale? You know, the one from that Wicca group you used to be in? She was great.   —X

October 8, 2002

I'm back in Sunnydale. On the bright side, I didn't go all veiny and homicidal! On the other side, I kind of turned myself invisible. Not to everyone, just to my friends, but... yeah, definitely did an accidental disappearing act as soon as I stepped off the plane.

It wouldn't have been such a big deal if there hadn't been a monster on the loose—after all, it's not the first time one of us has been invisible. That just made it an eventful Tuesday. But because wearing your Tuesday underwear in Sunnydale means that there's also probably something out there that wants to kill you, I was almost eaten by a parasitic skin-slurping, blood-lapping, mojo-resistant, singsongy demon thing named Gnarl. If Buffy and Xander hadn't used a kind-of-crazy, suddenly souled Spike to help track us to Gnarl's cave, I definitely would be dead.

Buffy killed Gnarl, as Buffy does. And I figured out the whole invisibility thing must have just been a subconscious spell that came from me thinking that I wasn't ready to see my friends again. Everyone was very forgiving—of this and of... the other thing. But Buffy admitted that she couldn't help but think that it might have been me skinning all Gnarl's victims, the way I skinned Tara's mur... Warren.

> What if you lost your Tuesday underwear and are instead wearing your Wednesday underwear three days a week? Does it still call demons? Is **THIS** why someone might become a demon magnet? Asking for a friend. —X

I don't blame her. I thought it might be, too. I mean, if I have the power to up and accidentally turn myself invisible, couldn't I be doing other, darker things by accident as well? If I start thinking about going dark too much, I start to feel paralyzed. Again. Only this isn't your fun, everyday demon-venom type of paralysis. This is the 100 percent pure Willow social anxiety type.

I don't know if I can do this; I can't even walk into our old bedroom without hearing the gunshot and feeling echoes of the rage I felt that day, as if all my despair has sunk into the carpet and the curtains and the bedding like a blood stain. Buffy gave me her room without my even having to ask. She came in while I was trying—and failing—to heal myself using the natural methods the coven had taught me, and she let me draw on her strength. Not five minutes later, my cuts were healed and my body was humming with power. And before I caught myself and stopped, I was thinking of ways to use that trick, to enhance it, to turn it into a weapon.

> You can. —B

I don't know if I can do this.

> You will. —B

HEALING SPELL
(OR, A SPELL TO TRANSFER ENERGIES TO THE SITE OF A DEMON-INFLICTED WOUND)

TOOLS AND INGREDIENTS:

ONE SUPERPOWERED SLAYER

Directions:

Close your eyes and relax into a state of meditation. Focus on your heart chakra and direct its energy to the site of your wound. Visualize the wounds closing.

When that doesn't work, have your Slayer friend come sit on your bed. Join hands. Get a boost of Chosen One power.

It's a whole lot better than ointment.

October 22, 2002

Buffy almost killed Anya today. Anya had called a spider demon to wreak havoc on a fraternity house (did I mention Anya became a vengeance demon again?), and it left a path of heartless bodies in its wake. If I hadn't used D'Hoffryn's talisman and called on him to intervene, I don't know what would have happened—Buffy had already clicked into Slayer mode. She has to, I get it. She'll need to be able to do that whenever the thing that's waiting to come up from beneath us decides to make its move.

> Thank you. For what it's worth.
> —A

Sometimes, though, it can be a little scary... you know, considering that I recently went off the good-guy roller coaster and onto the sidetrack of evil. Buffy insisted that the situation was different because I was human. But I have to admit, I don't always feel human anymore. When I was in that frat house this morning, and I had to call on old magick to protect me and that girl I found cowering in the closet, I didn't feel human. I felt... other.

D'Hoffryn noticed it, too. He still wants to recruit me to the side of vengeance. Says I have a gift for it. There's a part of me that leaps at the compliment, like he's my second-grade teacher and I just got an "A" on my spelling test. I don't know how to get rid of that part of me; ever since I can remember, I've always wanted to know everything, to be the smartest cookie in the cookie shop. When you're seven, that means knowing how to spell "Mississippi." When you're twenty-two and a recovering dark witch, the stakes are so much higher.

> What if you are twenty-three and still don't know how to spell "Mississippi" OR be a dark witch? (And yes—thanks, Will.)
> —X

If I lose control, if I become what I was, will Buffy find a loophole for me? Or will I have to be another "I killed Angel" story, the kind she tells to prove that she can do what's needed when the time comes?

> Sometimes it frightens me that Xander is in charge of power tools.
> —G

A Spell to Summon a Demon Via the Use of a Talisman
(In This Case, the Head Honcho of Vengeance)

Tools and Ingredients:
- Powder of Beleth
- Talisman of the demon you hope to summon

Directions:
Using the powder of Beleth, draw on the ground the symbol of the demon you would like to call—in this case, the symbol of D'Hoffryn.

Clasping the appropriate talisman between your hands, recite the following incantation:

> **Beatum sit in nominee** (insert name of demon, in this case **D'Hoffryn**).
>
> **Fiat hoc spatium porta ad mundum** (insert name of location where the demon resides, in this case the sunny burn of **Arashmaharr**).

Translation:

> I long to be in the presence of **D'Hoffryn**.
>
> Let this space become a portal to **Arashmaharr**.

While there are some demons that require fancier summoning gifts, most will respond in some measure to the basic ritual (even if they get a little grumpy).

RJ + WILLOW

I'm surprised you didn't make this entry disappear, Will. —B

Tempting. So, so tempting. But I realized that if we're operating under the same rule that lets the Dark Veiny Willow chapters stay in as a cautionary tale, Attempted De-Peening Spell probably fall somewhere in the same category. —W

NOVEMBER 5, 2002

I miss Tara. I don't think that I'm ever going to stop missing Tara. But for the first time since she's been gone, I felt a burst of something I never thought I'd feel again. Sure, from the outside, it might appear like inappropriate lust for a minor of the wrong gender, but I promise you: As soon as I do this spell to make R.J. not have a penis anymore, our love will be beautiful.

I can't believe we thought Buffy and Dawn were under a love spell; as if R.J., with his soft, golden hair and aura like a cloud of glittering sex butterflies, would ever need to stoop so low. Some people have a natural charisma that can't be contained.

The others have all run off to prove their affection with insignificant gestures. There was a moment when Buffy and I were rooting around in the basement for supplies—mine magickal and hers Principal Wood–killing—that I wanted to say, "Buffy come on. Put down that bazooka, and let's talk. In all our years of being friends, have we ever let a guy come between us? Sure, that's mostly because I'm gay and you have overcomplicated relationships with vampires, but why should we break our streak now?"

But then I realized that we'd just been waiting for the right guy to come along and get between us, a guy with wisdom beyond his years and eyelashes that are really more suited for a woman, anyway.

There's really no way to do this spell other than to call on Hecate. I just hope she's not too mad after all the times I tried to get her to de-rat Amy. She can get a little cranky.

Hey. I also had overcomplicated relationship with a secret Army agent who was vaguely superhu[man] because of all th[e] experiments the government was conducting on h[im]. Don't I get any credit for that? And I knew I sh[ould] have gotten rid o[f] that bazooka. —B

Would have been nice to get a "Hey, Dawn, don't go lie on the train tracks" speech. Just saying. —D

And you could have told me not to rob that... write that stupid poem. —A

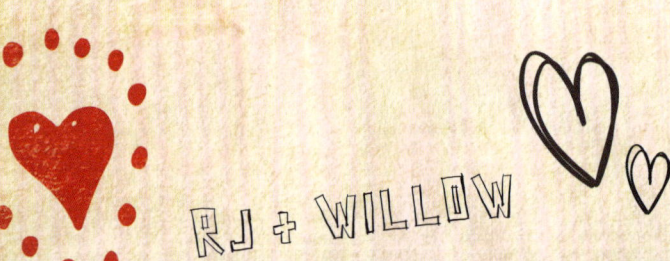

RJ + WILLOW

A Spell to Reverse a Person's Gender

Tools and Ingredients:
- Rose Quartz Crystals (4)
- Clear Quartz Crystals (4)
- Photo of the one you want to transform
- Copper Bowl
- Ginseng Oil
- White Candles (4)
- Nectar of a Peach

RJ + Willow

Directions:

Place the candles in a square. Position your copper bowl—with the clear quartz crystals inside—at the center, and scatter the rose quartz around the outside. Add a drop of ginseng oil, then the nectar of the peach.

As the quartz crystals rise and begin to swirl around you, say:

Oh Hecate, I call on you,

I humbly ask your will be done.

Hear my request,

A simple change,

Create a daughter from a son.

Still think he's pretty cute. —D

I am delighted to say that I don't. —B

Me either. —A

Me . . . three-ther. But he does have girly eyelashes. —W

November 16, 2002

We have a name for the thing that has been tormenting us from beneath ... only surprise! It's not so much from "beneath" anymore, and more from "before." It's the First Evil, and it's been playing with us. It pretended to have a message from Tara, it pretended to be Joyce's ghost and talked to Dawn, and who knows how long it's been talking to Spike—Buffy just thought he was talking to invisible people in the basement because of the soul situation. Instead, it's been slowly turning him into a weapon.

Buffy tried to cut through the fog and see if we could use Spike to figure out more about yet another baddie trying to get their apocalypse on, but no dice. That night we were attacked by Bringers, who seem to be the First's eyeless minions, and they took Spike. Buffy is determined to get him back, but if you try to pin down why, she'll change the subject. I learned a long time ago that trying to go down the Spike road is a sure way to get Buffy to go into closed-off Slayer mode, so I haven't pushed. Lately, she seems so brittle that even Xander is leaving it alone.

So we're left with not a lot of answers, and the one person who could potentially give us some—Andrew—is not much with the forthcoming-ness. Oh, did I mention that Andrew Wells is here? I ran into him while going to get blood for Spike, and for a second my vision went black and the dark spells, the ones that are still a part of me no matter what I've tried to do to purge them, flashed

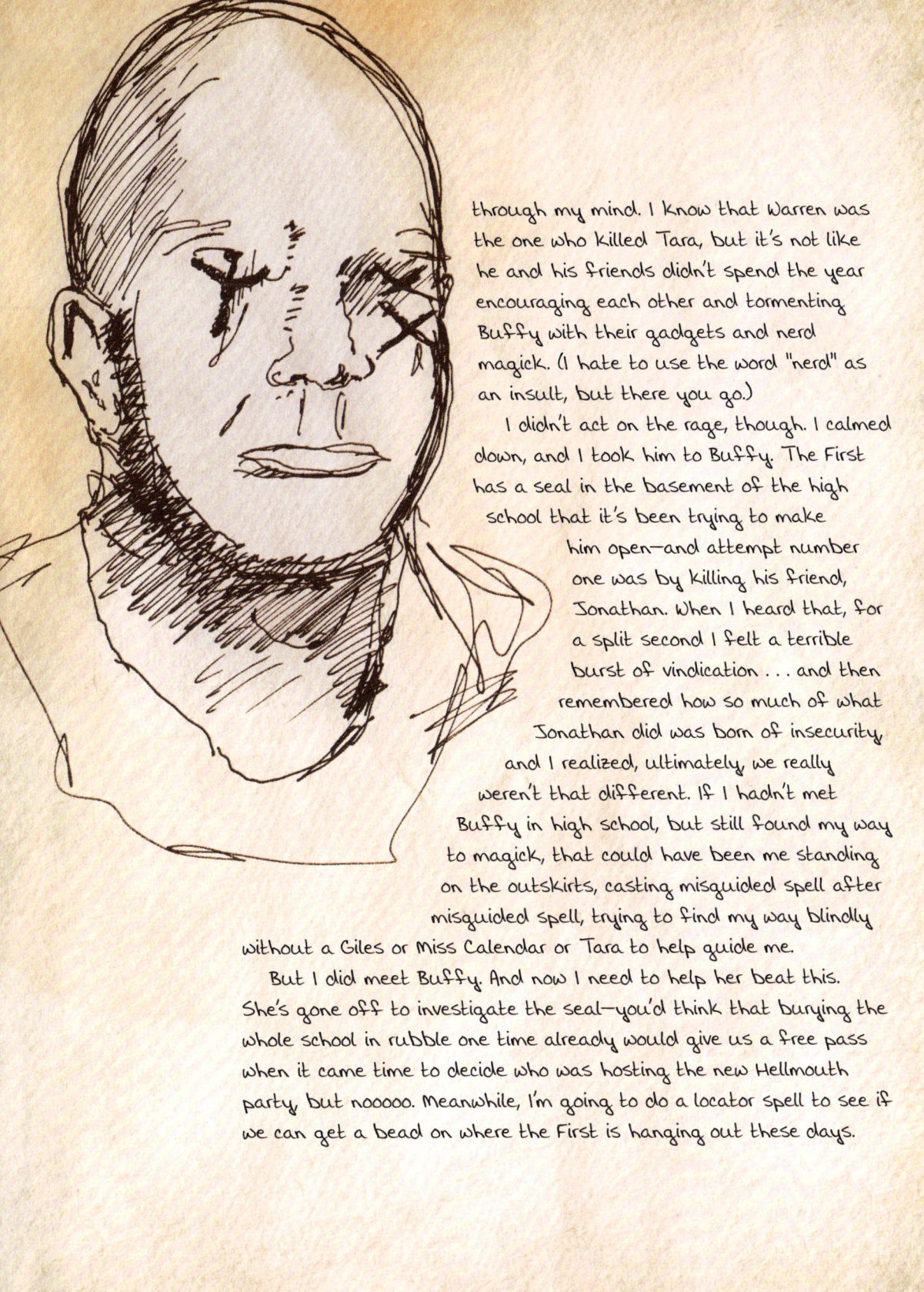

through my mind. I know that Warren was the one who killed Tara, but it's not like he and his friends didn't spend the year encouraging each other and tormenting Buffy with their gadgets and nerd magick. (I hate to use the word "nerd" as an insult, but there you go.)

I didn't act on the rage, though. I calmed down, and I took him to Buffy. The First has a seal in the basement of the high school that it's been trying to make him open—and attempt number one was by killing his friend, Jonathan. When I heard that, for a split second I felt a terrible burst of vindication . . . and then remembered how so much of what Jonathan did was born of insecurity and I realized, ultimately, we really weren't that different. If I hadn't met Buffy in high school, but still found my way to magick, that could have been me standing on the outskirts, casting misguided spell after misguided spell, trying to find my way blindly without a Giles or Miss Calendar or Tara to help guide me.

But I did meet Buffy. And now I need to help her beat this. She's gone off to investigate the seal—you'd think that burying the whole school in rubble one time already would give us a free pass when it came time to decide who was hosting the new Hellmouth party, but nooooo. Meanwhile, I'm going to do a locator spell to see if we can get a bead on where the First is hanging out these days.

A Spell to Locate the First Evil

I've tweaked my usual locator recipe and turned my usual evil dial up to eleven. Given that the First isn't exactly a demon, it's going to need a little work. It's more like summoning a spirit than anything else, although you remove the protective ingredients and leave out the steps to diminish the negative energy that attracts malignant spirits.

Tools and Ingredients:

- Map of Sunnydale
- Glass bowl
- Mugwort
- Spirit money
- Candles

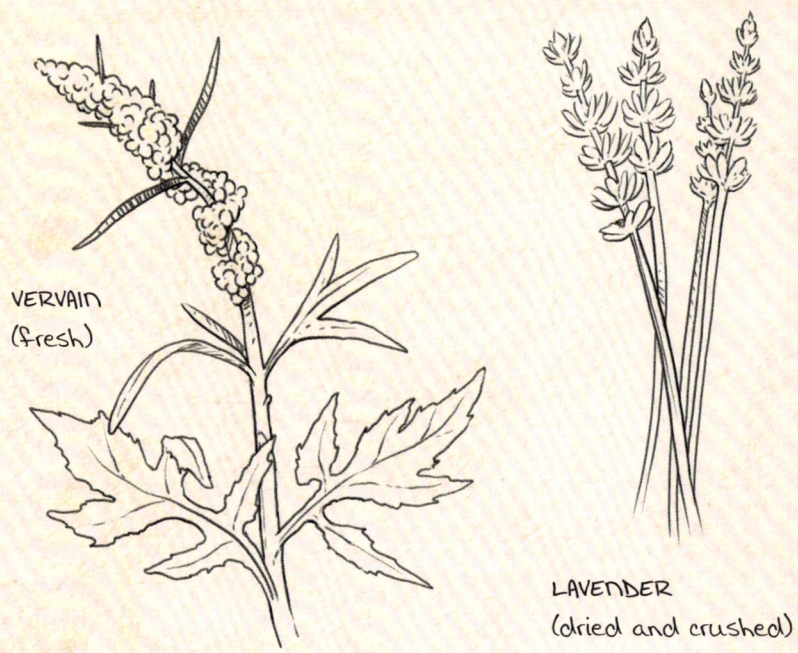

VERVAIN (fresh)

LAVENDER (dried and crushed)

Directions:

Spread your map out on a flat surface. Combine the vervain, mugwort, and spirit money in your glass bowl and set the mixture aflame. This is the offering that will call the essence of spirits to you as you ask to be shown the one you seek.

Light your candles. Pour the crushed lavender around the area you would like to plumb for negative spiritual activity. Say the following:

> Hades, open your door,
>
> Show us your first child.
>
> With your knowledge, may we see
>
> The darkness in his heart.

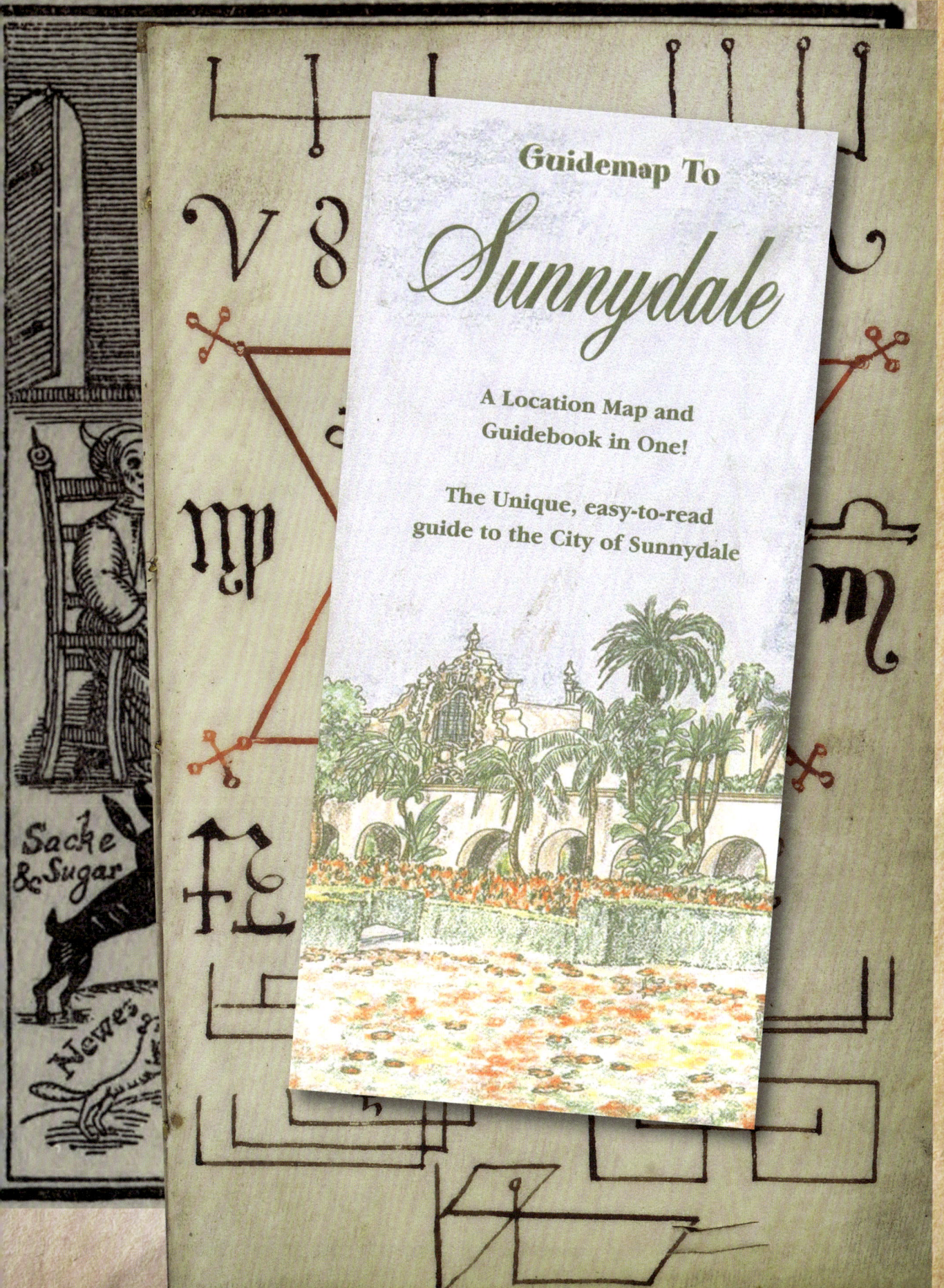

December 17, 2002

I didn't even get to finish the locator spell. The First showed up before I could start the incantation, inhabited my body, and took hold of my power to lash out at Buffy. I couldn't control it—and, with all that evil flowing through my veins, I didn't want to control it. I haven't felt that way since . . .

We know what the First wants now. Not too long after I did my best <u>Exorcist</u> impression, Giles showed up at our door, three strange girls in tow. He told us that they were potential Slayers, and that they were in danger of being eliminated now that the First Evil has made it his unholiest of unholy missions to eradicate the Slayer line and take over Earth, starting with the Hellmouth. Its agent for doing so is a monster called a Turok-Han. And if the black-and-blue Buffy who came back last night after trying to fight one is any indication, they are nothing like the cuddly, fluffy, murder-y kind of vampire that we've come to know and love here in Sunnydale.

I've never seen her looking so thrashed or so defeated. She's been trying to stay optimistic for our new Slayerette houseguests—and for Giles, but he's really more of an occasional houseguest who only shows up when things are super gloomy. She's determined to beat the First and its Turok-Han, and gave a whole speech last night about it choking on her and ripping hearts out. I admit I kind of tuned a lot of it out because I was too busy trying to get the chalky aftertaste of evil out of my mouth and whirling into my own pit of fear about how if she's serious about this, I'm going to have to forget that the most successful spell I've done since being back was to almost turn a guy into a girl.

She wants to fight a Turok-Han in front of the potentials, to show them that they can win. She's going to let it try to attack her and then lead it to a place where she'll trap it and kill it. I'm supposed to do a spell that will slow it down, which is . . . easier said than done. Given what baddies these übervamps are, I know what kind of spell I need to use—but it's dark. It would be easy to tweak the paralysis spell from when I went up against Glory to stop a forged-deep-in-the-earth kind of evil. But it's not a simple locator spell, or something from the natural magick kiddie pool I've been paddling in since I came back from England.

I'm worried. I just hope I can pull away when it's time.

> I also send flowers for weddings and greeting cards for . . . other developments.
> —G

How to Paralyze an Ancient Evil

Whereas the paralysis spell I used on Glory called upon the gorgon's power itself, this one calls upon the goddess who created the gorgon—Minerva—in the hope that she will use her gifts of strategy in battle to aid us in this fight.

PIECE OF OBSIDIAN (carved with a pentagram)

Tools and Ingredients:
- LAPIS LAZULI (for wisdom)

Directions:
Hold the obsidian in your left hand, the lapis lazuli in your right.

Offer the following supplication:

> Caerimonia Minerva,
> Ut vocant, in sapientia tua,
> Nam exspectando certamen.
> Salva virtute,
> Acuunt vestra arma.

Translation:
> Blessed Minerva,
> We call on your wisdom
> For the upcoming battle.
> Save your strength,
> Hone your weapon.

When you are ready for the barrier to go up, say the second part of the incantation:

> Caerimonia Minerva,
> Saepio, saepire, saepsi.
> Saepio impedimentum!

Translation:
> Blessed Minerva,
> Who defended, is defending, will defend.
> Defend us now!

January 21, 2003

Buffy's taking the junior Slayer team out for a super special "Learn to Be a Slayer" date with a freshly rescued Spike so they'll be prepared if another Turok-Han comes after us. Of course, it's not like she thought to ask me or anything. I know I'm not an official potential, but given how much macaroni and cheese I've been cooking for their stupid pre-supernatural appetites—only some of it extra crunchy—you'd think that I could at least have gotten a pity invite. She even considered letting Andrew go. She argued with him about it, but I could tell that if he had pressed a little bit more she might have caved. She had her "I'm Going to Cave I'm Just Being a Pain in the Butt Because I Can" face on.

But whatever. I'm fine here with Willow and Andrew, I guess. I beat Andrew at a video game, so I guess I'm a potential nerd, if nothing else. We're also getting ready to help Willow do a spell to locate the soon-to-be-Slayer that Willow's Dial-a-Coven says is right here in Sunnydale.

I asked Willow if I could do the writing down of things, and she said sure. She's kind of distracted lately—I think one of the potentials, Kennedy, has been flirting with her. I don't know that I like Kennedy all that much, but I might be biased because Kennedy always wakes up early and eats all the good cereal before I have a chance to get to it. I also don't think that there's anyone as perfect for Willow as Tara.

> Burnt. You mean burnt. But given my spam experiments, I shouldn't throw stones. I will, but I shouldn't. —A

> I wasn't going to cave. You must have been mistaking my "I'm Trying Not to Tie You to a Chair Again" face for it. You know the one. AND you could have come. You didn't ask. —B

> I'd wager that's just your face. —S

    Willow just asked me if I've been paying attention to the ingredients that she's been pulling out of her bag. I nodded, but I maybe missed one. And anyway, even though Willow doesn't like people to look at her grimoire or whatever it is, I've seen her go to town when it comes to the journaling, so I'm just doing the real witch thing, the same way that I've been chipping in with the research and the Scoobying when duty calls. They don't think I know how to do what they do, but I've spent years watching it. Even if only two of those years are real years and not monk-sponsored years, I think I'm still pretty much an expert.

    I could probably even do a better job at potential slaying than a lot of these girls who have been showing up. I've watched them training down in the basement, and the other day, I saw Vi stake some shifty-looking laundry detergent instead of the target. They also seem to be nervous about everything, whereas I've survived two apocalypses, including the one that I . . . guess I technically caused? I didn't really have a say, though—so, not my fault? I don't know.

    Anyway, Willow is telling me to write down the directions because if it works, she'll put it in her book. I said, "It seems like you kind of just throw stuff in the fire and say a poem," but she says she wants it to be a little more detailed than that, so . . . oops.

    Wouldn't it be kind of cool if I was the potential? I mean, it would also be scary. But then I'd finally know that I was here for something other than just to open a gateway that's been sealed over.

Dawnie, I knew you weren't paying attention. I wrote it down for you. —W

A Spell to Locate a Potential Slayer

TOOLS AND INGREDIENTS:

- EGG
- TUMBLEWEED
- SNAKE SKIN
- ROSEBUSH THORN
- CHRYSALISSES (CHRYSALI?)

DIRECTIONS:

Say the incantation below. Upon naming each ingredient, throw it into a crucible of roaring flame hotter than Mount Doom. (It's really just a fireplace—Andrew helped with that last part.)

> To light the aura of the new,
>
> Skin of snake and chrysalis, too.
>
> To indicate the fresh reborn,
>
> Tumbleweed and rosebush thorn.
>
> An egg that means life to come,
>
> Take this, oh spirits, and my spell is done.

It should create a cloud that will attach to the new Slayer you seek, much like a symbiote attaches to Spider-Man. (Also Andrew.)

JANUARY 31, 2003

Dawn's not wrong—Kennedy has been making eyes at me. But next time I'm going to be a little more specific about what the parameters are for writing quest spells.

There is a reason that I haven't been writing about Kennedy here. I'd be lying if I said I wasn't somewhat flattered by her take-no-prisoners flirting style. No one's ever pursued me like that; my relationships always happened gradually—so gradually that sometimes I didn't even know they were happening at all. And yet Kennedy is like "Hey, I just met you but I think you have very lickable freckles." She's the exact opposite of Tara, and I should hate that. I do hate that. But there's also been a small part of me that says I should just give in and go with it.

So I went with it. I let her woo me with her fruity umbrella drinks and her kisses. Worse, I enjoyed them both . . . at least until we stopped kissing and realized that I had turned into Warren Mears.

I turned into Tara's killer.

It turns out that it was all because of Amy. She put a hex on me, and that's the reason that my magick has been going all kerflooey and I went invisible upon returning to Sunnydale. The penance malediction was designed to latch onto the deepest, darkest thoughts that pass through my mind and inspire self-inflicted spells.

I turned into Warren because I thought kissing Kennedy meant that I was letting Tara go. I still feel like maybe it is, but I think I also know that Tara wouldn't want me to feel so guilty about being close to another person. She wouldn't want me to be alone forever. She wasn't like that.

I don't know what's going to happen with Kennedy. I don't even know if we're all going to be alive next week. But it does feel nice to know that Kennedy is looking out for me. She was even able to nab some of Amy's papers before Amy poofed her back into our backyard.

I'm including Amy's spell here because who knows if it's still spidering away in my subconscious. Amy is kind of an evil genius. I mean, she's also a heinous bitch who will need to buy another hamster wheel if I ever see her again, but an evil genius all the same. I guess the twisted-sister apple doesn't fall far from the twisted-sister tree. Just goes to show you that you should never lend someone your hairbrush.

> I get this. I mean, the giving in and going with it part. But trade flirty umbrellas for demon bars and rock operas and . . . can I cross this out? I'm crossing this out. She seems nice . . . in a, you know, tiny and aggressive way. And you deserve to be happy. Tara would want it. —B

> Let me know if you want to borrow a highlighter for this part, Buffy. —D

Wanna hear something funny? I slip up and do a teensy-weensy time spell that causes my dad to lose his job and I get kicked out of the house and told "not to come back if I'm going to keep up that Catherine crap". Willow almost destroys the world? Sure, let's welcome her back into the fold with open arms.

I'm sure that she thinks her magick is under control, so why not make things a little interesting. Maybe people won't be so forgiving if her powers get a little dangerous. And the best part? Her subconscious will choose the perfect weapon.

A HEX TO PREY ON ONE'S SUBCONSCIOUS
(Penance Malediction)   by Amy

REQUIREMENTS:
A SLIP OF PAPER (with the victim's name written in blood)
A LOCK OF WILLOW'S HAIR
LIVE SPIDER (any variety)
BETEL NUT
ASAFETIDA POWDER
CAULDRON

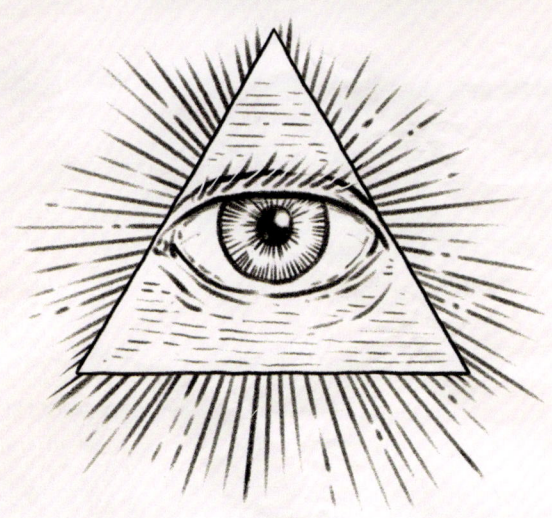

Using your asafetida powder, draw the symbol of the conscious eye large enough that a cauldron can be placed in its pupil. Add the hair, paper, live spider, and betel nut. As the mixture smokes and hisses, say the following:

> Cherished child, oft forgiven,
> I curse you with a life so riven.
> By betel nut and spider's crawl,
> Let chaos enter at your mind's call.
> I point the ancient law against thee,
> Let what you wrought come back in three.
> And when you feel thou are forsaken,
> Let you know it is of your own makin'.

The betel nut should still be intact. Draw it out, and then bury it outside on a moonless night. The spell will have an impact as long as the nut still holds some form, or as long as the victim is unaware that it has been cast.

FEBRUARY 18, 2003

We know the name of what we're fighting; we know what it wants; but we still don't have any way of defeating it. I've gone over this book a hundred times, trying to see if there's something that I missed, some spell I could build on, but so far . . . nothing. That's why I decided to share it. Selectively, of course—I don't really have any desire to let what's-her-name who's always eating cereal in the kitchen in on how I once almost destroyed the world. But I swallowed my embarrassment and opened it up to the people I trust. I just had to be out of the room and out of the range of anything pointy when I saw them reading it.

Unfortunately, it didn't seem to get us anywhere, so the Summers house has officially become Slayer training central. You can't go two feet without hearing a "Hiyah!" or the sound of some sort of weapon thunking into a piece of wood. Giles has been racking up the frequent-flier miles collecting new potentials from all over the world, and Dawn and I have been staying up until 3 a.m. getting research and brushing up on our rusty translation skills. Andrew even programmed the new microwave.

And yet, it's not enough for Buffy. One of the girls, Chloe, killed herself the other night, a victim of the First finding its way into her head. Buffy took it hard, and this time she projected that bundle of Slayer rage outward, telling us that we weren't doing enough to help her fight the First. Kennedy mounted a defense, mouthing off that Buffy wasn't even the most powerful person in the room, but I nipped that in the bud, even though a tiny voice inside of me whispered that Kennedy may have had a point. But power is only power if you can use it and count on it not turning you into a maniacal supervillain. Buffy may be intense, but she's never lost touch with what is right.

I thought if we laid low, Buffy would cool down and go back to the only slightly unpredictable-under-stress version we know and love. Instead, she dragged us all into watching a creepy mystical puppet show about the origins of the First Slayer and then hopped in a magick door. And we were all left to figure out how to get her back, not to mention deal with the demon that we'd been gifted with "in exchange." Thanks so much for the trial by fire, Buff!

It worked, though, as long as by "worked" you mean I went Scary Willow and sucked the life energy out of my (sort of?) girlfriend without even a "Hey, you cool with this?" I tried to apologize to Kennedy afterward, but she was too unnerved by what happened to hear it. I get it. I do. And yet the fear on her face still stings.

Later, Buffy confessed that she thinks she made a mistake while she was off vacationing in Portal Land. Apparently the men who created the First Slayer offered her more power, but she didn't like that it made her less human. I couldn't help but feel a flash of anger. It must be nice to be able to make that decision, to not have someone asking you to risk your humanity again and again and again in service of a plan that you don't even get to initial.

But she's the Slayer, and she calls the shots. We have to trust her. Even if sometimes it seems like we're the ones making the sacrifices.

The Ritual of Reverse Exchange
(or, a spell to reopen the portal your slayer friend just threw herself in, all willy-nilly)

TOOLS AND INGREDIENTS:
- KRAKEN'S TOOTH
- BALTIC STONE (ground)
- SKIN OF DRACONIS
- THE SURPRISE DEMONIC EXCHANGE STUDENT WHO APPEARED AS SOON AS BUFFY HOPPED IN THE DOOR

(Note: Anya said we needed a conduit, and offered three suggestions. I thought, hey why not just go ahead and throw 'em all in there? See: Effort, last ditch).

DIRECTIONS:
Grind all three conduits together, until you have enough to complete a casting circle. Draw it on a flat surface, then sit in the middle and say the following request to open a portal:

	TRANSLATION:
VIA TEMPORIS	TIME,
I AM CLAMO AD TE	I CRY TO YOU.
VIA SPATTI	SPACE,
TE JUBEO APERIRE	I BID THEE OPEN.
APERI	OPEN.
VIA CONCURSUS	AT THIS INTERSECTION
TEMPUS, SPATIUM	OF BOTH,
AUDI ME UT IMPERIUM	LISTEN TO MY ORDER.

FEBRUARY 26, 2003

Xander got hurt. Buffy decided that she and the potentials needed to go after a new threat at an evil vineyard, half-cocked and research-free, and it turned out to be a trap. Caleb, the frocked bastard who was waiting there, stuck his finger in Xander's eye. Xander has been trying to put on a brave face—we both have—but we could barely even get through one round of joking at the hospital before I had to stop because of tears. We've both faced injuries in the line of duty before, but never something so permanent. Never something that I couldn't heal with magick if I really needed to.

The girls are mourning the death of two of their own. And they're scared of the Bad Guy Whack-a-Mole game that we can't seem to stop playing. But instead of sitting down and trying to understand where we're all coming from, Buffy is still barking orders—that is, when Buffy's present at all. She's barely come by the hospital since Xander's been injured, and when she does, she just rattles off everything the doctor said and then scampers off like an emotionally disconnected bunny.

We're trying to help her. And yet, somehow, when it comes time to make decisions, we don't have a voice and our team turns into a dictatorship. When our friends get injured—when our friends die—we're just supposed to say, "It's okay, Buffy. We know you tried your best. Some of us are broken and maimed, but I'm sure you'll get it right next time. Here, take my girlfriend into the line of fire. It's not like the last one was killed by someone who was aiming for you."

That's not fair. I know it's not fair. It's just that the other day, Kennedy—who I just called my girlfriend so I guess we're really dating now—and I were having yet another argument about the rightness and goodness of doing whatever Buffy said and suddenly I realized that I was just parroting my old part without really believing what I was saying.

Buffy asked Giles and me if we could work on getting more information on this Caleb character from the police. In all the chaos caused by people fleeing Sunnydale, their computer systems are down and unhackable, so I have to use a spell. I'm going to do it, because we're facing another apocalypse, but it hasn't escaped my notice that this is delving back into the not-quite-kosher area of magick.

A Spell to Make One Susceptible to Suggestion

(or, how to make Sunnydale's police force hand you the files you need about a certain evil preacher without asking too many questions)

TOOLS AND INGREDIENTS:
- PAPER
- LEATHER POUCH
- POKEROOT
- AGUEWEED

HEMATITE
("the stone of the mind")

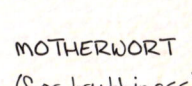

MOTHERWORT
(for truthiness)

DIRECTIONS:
Add the hematite, motherwort, agueweed, and pokeroot to a small leather gris-gris pouch. On a scrap of paper, write the following:

> A charm for truth telling, a charm for suggestion.
>
> Make thine enemies obey without question.

Enemies will be susceptible to influence as long as you carry the charm on your person and maintain eye contact.

155

March 1, 2003

Today we all decided that Buffy should take a little breather from the apocalypse. You know, get some much-needed rest and come back with a clearer head and more cooperative can-do spirit in the morning.

Oh God, it sounds just as lame in writing as it did when I tried to explain it to Spike after he got back from following up a lead on the weapon Buffy thinks Caleb is hiding. I think I messed up. I think we all messed up. It's just that Buffy calmly walked into the living room, stood in front of girls who had just lost a friend and a man who had just lost his eye, and told them that she was sending us all back to fight Caleb. Like it was no biggie. Like we were all just collateral damage, little pawns in a chess game that she alone has been deemed worthy to play.

When Kennedy challenged Buffy, I stepped in to defend her, as usual, but the words just wouldn't come.

It all spiraled out of control from there. The next thing I knew, Dawn was telling Buffy that she had to leave the house if she couldn't get on board with this new democracy (which, I kind of agree with Amanda, would work better if run according to parliamentary procedure rather than by popular vote). It seems that the potential Slayers don't have many former model UN members, however, because the equality was short-lived. Now we're all looking to Faith, of all people, who has gotten the girls to kidnap one of the eyeless Bringer guys so we can force him to talk.

Unfortunately, he has no tongue. Dawn mentioned a Turkish spell that can help you speak with those who are, for some reason, unable to do so. It should be easy enough to do—I just wish that I felt this confident about the decision we made to do this without Buffy.

A SPELL TO GIVE VOICE TO ONE WHO CANNOT SPEAK

Good when you kidnap someone with plans to smack him around for info but find out he's mute... I don't know how we're ever going to win this one.

TOOLS AND INGREDIENTS:
- LOBELIA POWDER
- BERGAMOT POWDER
- CHARCOAL
- CENSER

DIRECTIONS:

Hang a censer near the person you're hoping to make speak. After lighting the charcoal and letting it burn to ash, add the lobelia and bergamot powders and set the mixture to smolder.

As a light smoke fills the room, say the following:

> KENDINIZI ÇOK UYKULU
> HISSETMEYE BASHLIYORSUNUZ.
> ÇOK UYKULU, ÇOK UYKULU.
> GÖZLERINIZIN ÖNÜNDE
> SALLAMAK IÇIN CEP SAATIM
> YOK AMA, SIZIN DE
> GÖZLERINIZ YOK. KONUSUN
> BIZIMLE.

TRANSLATION:

> YOU ARE GETTING VERY SLEEPY.
> VERY, VERY SLEEPY. I DO
> NOT HAVE A POCKET WATCH, BUT
> THEN AGAIN, YOU DO NOT HAVE
> EYES. SPEAK TO US.

I couldn't find my translation, and Dawn's Turkish copy has an unfortunate and easily avoidable chocolate milkshake stain right over the incantation, so we had to wing it a little. If it works, the voice should find "its most willing host." Or it will find "a man with a giraffe." ... My Turkish is a little rusty.

A Spell to Share the Power of the Chosen One

Buffy was right all along: Caleb was trying to hide a weapon from us. She went back to the vineyard this morning, alone, to get it. And while she was kicking preacher butt, Faith led her group into a waiting horde of Turok-Hans.

No one's talking about what happened, least of all Buffy, but you can feel the ripple of relief that's come from having her back in charge—even Faith seems happy to wash her hands of the leadership, having really felt, for the first time, what it's like to be in Buffy's shoes. I think we all have a new understanding of that now. For me, when Buffy handed me her new, shiny, scythe-looking thing and told me to get with the research, it felt like an unspoken welcome back to the fold. And I never want to be unfolded again.

We don't know much about the new weapon, only that Buffy knows it contains the essence of her Slayer powers and that it predates written history. She asked me if I thought I could tap into that magick and share it with all the potentials—not just the ones in our house, but the undiscovered ones across the world. That way it will no longer be "she alone" who can stop the vampires, the demons, and the forces of darkness, but an army.

With evil slavering at our door, there was nothing I could say other than that I'll try. I'm terrified, though. I told Giles that I couldn't sense the scythe's power, but that wasn't true, not exactly. I could sense it, and I could tell right away that, at its heart, it's the same kind of intoxicating dark magick that made me lose control once before. Split among a legion of Slayers, it will give them strength; trapped in one selfish, insecure person, it could burn her from the inside out.

I've been scribbling plans all night. Kennedy says she'll be there the whole time to keep me grounded, which is sweet, but she doesn't really understand what I have to do. There are no ingredients, no charms, no supplies—there's just me. I need to absorb the scythe's power and then use the energetic web that connects all of humanity to find the Slayers. At first I was at a loss when it came to what I could draw on as a guide, but then it hit me.

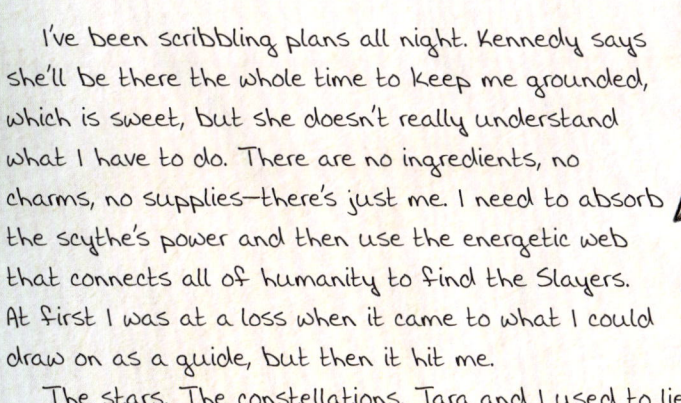

The stars. The constellations. Tara and I used to lie on our backs and look at them sometimes, me whispering their real names and her whispering the names that she had made up as a little girl: The Big Pineapple, The Little Pineapple, Short Man Looking Uncomfortable, Moose Getting a Sponge Bath, Little Pile of Crackers. It will be like she is there with me, too.

And so I write, and I reread my plans and diagrams, but the truth is that this isn't a test for which I can study. It's a weighing of my soul, a judgment of how far I've come. As all that power flows through my veins, I will have to decide to offer up everything I have for something that's bigger than me—willingly. There can be no ego. There can be no Old Willow, or New Willow, or Good-with-Computers Willow, or Sidekick Willow, or Dark Veiny Willow.

There just has to be a girl. One girl, in all the world, who wants to change it so that her friend doesn't have to fight alone anymore.

TITAN BOOKS

A division of Titan Publishing Group Ltd
144 Southwark Street
London SE1 0UP
www.titanbooks.com

Find us on Facebook: www.facebook.com/InsightEditions
Follow us on X: @insighteditions

Buffy the Vampire Slayer TM & © 2017 Twentieth Century Fox Film Corporation. All rights reserved.

Images on pages 28, 34, 35, 63, 69, 119, 145, 148, and 149 copyright Wellcome Library, London, supplied by Wellcome Collection, licensed under CC BY 4.0. Website: https://wellcomeimages.org/

Published by arrangement with Insight Editions, San Rafael, California.
www.insighteditions.com

No part of this publication may be reproduced, stored in a retrieval system, or transmitted, in any form or by any means without the prior written permission of the publisher, nor be otherwise circulated in any form of binding or cover other than that in which it is published and without a similar condition being imposed on the subsequent purchaser.

A CIP catalogue record for this title is available from the British Library.

EU RP (FOR AUTHORITIES ONLY)
eucomply OÜ Pärnu mnt 139b-14 11317,
Tallinn, Estonia
hello@eucompliancepartner.com, +3375690241

ISBN: 978-1-7856-5727-6

Publisher: Raoul Goff
Associate Publisher: Vanessa Lopez
Art Director: Chrissy Kwasnik
Designer: Jon Glick
Associate Editor: Courtney Andersson
Managing Editor: Alan Kaplan
Editorial Assistant: Tessa Murphy
Production Editor: Rachel Anderson
Production Manager: Alix Nicholaeff

Illustrations by Scott Buoncristiano

Insight Editions, in association with Roots of Peace, will plant two trees for each tree used in the manufacturing of this book. Roots of Peace is an internationally renowned humanitarian organization dedicated to eradicating land mines worldwide and converting war-torn lands into productive farms and wildlife habitats. Roots of Peace will plant two million fruit and nut trees in Afghanistan and provide farmers there with the skills and support necessary for sustainable land use.

Manufactured in China by Insight Editions

10 9 8 7 6 5

DISCLAIMER:
The stories and spells in this book are works of fiction. A. M. Robinson, Insight Editions, and Twentieth Century Fox expressly disclaim any responsibility for any adverse effects from the use or application of the information contained in this book. A. M. Robinson, Insight Editions, and Twentieth Century Fox shall not be liable for any losses suffered by any reader of this book.